To Sand

February 1986

With my very best wishes

THE POCKET GUIDE TO
TENNIS
TACTICS

John Crooke

John Crooke.

Shrewsbury.

If all pupils were as easy
to deal with (and mothers) I should
not look as old as I do on
page nine!

Bell & Hyman

The Pocket Guide to Tennis Tactics
was designed and edited by
Holland & Clark Limited, London

Designer
Julian Holland

Artist
Martin Smillie

Cover photo by Michael Cole Camerawork:
Carling Bassett

Photo Credits
Permission to use their photographs has been very kindly given by Adidas;
Mr Roger Hodge; Momentum Leisure (for Tacchini); Slazengers Ltd; Roger
Price Photographic Ltd.

Published by Bell & Hyman
Denmark House, 37/39 Queen Elizabeth Street,
London SE1 2QB

British Library Cataloguing in Publication Data
Crooke, John
    The pocket guide to tennis tactics.
    1. Tennis
    1. Title
    796.742'2   GV995

ISBN 0-7135-2540-1

Phototypeset in Great Britain by
Tradespools Limited, Frome, Somerset

Produced in Great Britain by
the Bath Press, Avon

Contents

Introduction

Even in this age of computers, it is still frequently a book which triggers off ideas. A book is an indispensable aid in self-teaching and you are probably reading this page because you wish to learn more about tennis tactics in order to become a more effective player on court.

Whatever your playing experience and intended commitment to tennis, this book can help you and your learning is possible in two ways. Precise instructions may be strictly followed or experiment may be made within a set of guidelines.

The first method is quicker and suits a book's style but any firmly changed response, developed by the second method, is usually more secure. This volume tries to combine both methods.

Countless pieces of tennis information, advice and folklore will already be stored away in your mind and this book attempts to retrieve, organize and supplement, that tactical knowledge.

Whether it succeeds in this aim is largely up to you.

Note

For the sake of simplicity, the text refers throughout to a right-handed male player but, except where specifically stated, all the advice applies equally to left-handers and to female players.

Right: Single out the right tactic and be doubly effective.

Objectives and Definitions

Objectives
Most tennis players have three objectives. First, to win – or at least to acquit themselves well in response to a challenge. Secondly, to enjoy the process of winning, or of responding to tougher and tougher situations. Thirdly, to live that little more fully via involvement in tennis.

Main Reasons for Playing
Reasons for playing will vary from person to person, but will probably be an amalgam of the following, depending on age, outlook and skill potential.

★ For younger enthusiasts, tennis can be a way of going high in the sporting world – with all the demands and rewards entailed.
★ The game is a way of widening social contacts.
★ It is a pleasant and basically healthy pastime.
★ There are challenges to intelligence, nerve and physical capacities.
★ There is a pleasurable satisfaction in making rhythmical and polished responses to the ball within the permitted limits of tennis.
★ Depending on your age, you may be playing at the insistence or encouragement of parent or spouse – tennis being considered the least of the many evils that could befall you.

Personal Objectives
You will know – or you will need to identify – where you stand in relation to these reasons for playing. The aim of this book is to assist you in achieving your personal objectives more readily and regularly.

Objectives of Competitive Tennis
Irrespective of these *personal objectives*, the objectives of competitive tennis are clear, simple and unchanging. They are:
1 **To restrict your own errors.**
2 **To force opponents into errors.**

If your current playing standard is low, say weak club team and below, then the first objective – restricting your own errors – is of the higher importance. If your current playing standard is higher, good club team/weakish county and above, then forcing errors from an opponent is of prime importance.

Definitions
Grand strategy is the planning of your overall tennis life, or 'season' and involves many off-court factors.
Strategy is your overall plan of campaign for a match, or a linked series of matches.
Tactics are your on court moves and counter-moves (via the ball and the feet) in each developing situation.

Strategy and tactics require objectives. Such objectives must be achievable within an appropriate time and should be reasonably measurable – after all you will want to know whether you have actually won that coveted title or not!

Tactics
Tactics are influenced by three factors: You; Your Opponent; and the Environment. The first leg of this three-legged stool is *You*. Tennis *demands* the same from everyone, but according to age, experience, standard, physique, intelligence and motivation, the *response* varies.

It would obviously be disastrous for a heavy once-a-week doubles player to plan to win a rare singles encounter with a younger, fitter opponent by fleetness of foot about the court and by the application of unremitting pressure. Judicious placing of the first shot in each encounter, coupled with a limitation of angles, and broken by high-risk adventurous hitting for winners when opportunities occur, might well pay greater dividends and be better than risking a spell in an intensive-care ward after indulging in overlong rallies.

Similarly, a short, rather nervous and shy girl with considerable ballet training is not playing very intelligently if she bases her game on big, killing first services and all-out power placements on return of service.

Your tactics must primarily exploit to the full your two greatest assets – *your* brain and *your* body.

Above: the author defending desperately and counting his tactical options on his fingers!

What Type of Player Are You?

There is no universal 'right' way to play a stroke or a match – the most effective stroke must be employed each time and tactics chosen to suit the situation. Remember that an umpire's pencil, making dots on the score sheet, cannot distinguish between exquisite beauty of stroke production and crudely functional racket-work.

Discovering the type of player you are (or could be) is the first step. Go through the checklist below and analyse your game as honestly as possible. Your answers could deceive others but you will only cheat yourself if you try for an 'acceptable' answer instead of the honest response. Writing down your replies is an important part of this exercise.

1. What is the dominant pattern of your game?
Allowing for the considerable gap in playing standard, consider any top players you happen to have seen (probably on TV) and check for similarities with your game.
Aggressive A player attempting to dominate short, power-packed, quick-fire rallies and gaining net command whenever possible on any surface. Pam Shriver, Pat Cash and Jimmy Connors typify this approach. Such players hit hard but very accurately.
All-round A player prepared to rally from the baseline on slower surfaces but eager to finish off a point at the net.

Martina Navratilova and John McEnroe are good left-handed examples. McEnroe nudges and flicks endlessly at a ball from the baseline

What Type of Player are You?
A. Powerfully built but quick?
B. Solid and determined?
C. Short and tough?
D. Tall with long reach?
E. Frail and inexperienced?
F. Thin but totally concentrated and composed?

A

B

C

E

D

F

but suddenly turns an interminable rally by a shot which opens up a quick kill at the net.

The right-hander, Ivan Lendl, hits even harder in baseline exchanges but is prepared to make and take reasonable net-command opportunities.

Defensive Players such as Chris Evert Lloyd or Mats Wilander, who are prepared to scheme patiently from their baseline treadmill, answering pace with stealth and consistency but able to hit hard and volley effectively when appropriate.

(There are numerous sub-divisions but you should be able to identify with one of these players.)

2. Do you dictate the play?

Or are you more of a responder, or perhaps a little of both. Think carefully – this is not quite the same as Question One.

An aggressive player is not always dictating. He or she might be merely responding to the situation, or to an opponent's ploys. On the other hand, a defensive player might not always be responding, but be deliberately setting up defensive situations to trap a wild, unwary attacker.

3. Do you wish to control the ball totally?

Are you prepared to lower the pace of the game considerably in order to achieve this end?

Or are you attempting aggressive penetration right from the start – even though it would frequently be more prudent to build up to a knock-out blow?

4. What is your physique?

Are you: short or tall? Fast or slow about the court? Fit or unfit for long matches?

5. Which is more important to you?

The sheer pleasure of hitting a ball (well) about the court; or winning the contest against another human being?

6. Which of these descriptions would fit you most closely?

* A natural player.
* An inspirational player.
* A manufactured player.
* A workmanlike player.
* A cerebral player.

7. Do you still perform effectively and frequently win even on your off days?

8. Are you a player who regularly rises to the occasion?

9. Do you try very early in a match to adapt your game to the surface and/or your opponent?

10. Do you endeavour to play 100% of the game 100% well, or do you try to play 50% of the game 100% well?

11. In how many of these situations do you feel really confident?

* About to deliver a first service.
* About to receive any service.
* About to play a forehand cross-court drive off an easy ball.
* About to play a backhand cross-court drive off an easy ball.
* About to play a crisp, high volley at the net.

★ About to play a real opponent-stranding drop-shot.

★ About to play a lob in a 50/50 situation (ie not in desperate defence).

★ About to play any drive imparting topspin.

★ About to play any drive imparting slice.

12. Is this the first time you have done any real analysis of your play?

It would be an unusually insensitive player who did not have some broad idea of the *type* of player he was, but the checklist might have sharpened the focus on your game, *especially if you were confusing the player you would like to be with the player you are.*

If your ideal player is markedly different from that earnest tennis being who turns out for matches in your tennis-wear and shoes and using your racket, then probably very considerable technical change and long physical preparation are required. In other words, you cannot become a big server and sharp volleyer just by wishing strongly enough for it and absorbing the theory.

To become a 'big server' you could well have to modify the way in which you hold your racket and the manner in which you build your racket-head throw at the ball. In addition, it could take years for the back muscles and other muscle groups to develop the required strength and flexibility. If you are under the age of 40 and dedicated, all this is possible, but most people

will not wish tennis to dominate their lifestyle to that extent.

Consequently, the objective of this book is to assist in making the most of what you already have; to get your actual performance and achievement nearer to your *personal potential high level*, without radical changes to your technique and lifestyle.

Rest assured, it is there within you – higher effectiveness on court is there for the asking, but, like any good general (or businessman) you must use your resources and assets sensibly and to your maximum advantage.

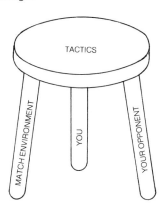

Your Opponent
The second leg of the stool is your opponent. What he is trying to do will affect your tactics – especially if he gets in first. More obviously, if your favourite tactic were to make the opponent run extensively and you came against a marathon-jogger who revelled in scampering about a court all day, you would need to do some re-thinking.

Therefore, your opponent will exert considerable influence on your initial and subsequent tactical decisions, but that is definitely not the same as allowing the opponent to master you and to take the initiative.

The Environment

This is covered more explicitly on pp 64–73, but again it is logical that the surface, the weather, the venue, the background, the occasion and the mood (yours, your opponent's and your colleagues') will all subtly influence matters on court.

To take a simple example – on a slow surface and on a calm day it might not be productive to serve riskily fast and then try, in long protracted rallies, to manoeuvre all over the court an agile and fit opponent who has consistent, nagging accuracy. However, against the same opponent and on the same court, but now slippery and fast after rain and with a capricious wind, such tactics might well be more effective.

Conclusions

Your tactics should therefore be:

1. Clear and simple but definitely *not* unchanging.

2. Appropriate. They should reflect what you are best at doing, what your opponent is weakest at doing, and what fits the prevailing conditions best.

3. Practised in less challenging situations.

4. Imaginative. Remember that to be clear and simple in intent does not necessarily mean to be commonplace.

Diagram 1

TAKING THE CORRECT
TACTICAL STEPS

CONSOLIDATION FOR FUTURE

EXPERIENCE GAINED MUST INFLUENCE FUTURE PLANNING & LEVEL ACHIEVED MUST BE PLATFORM FOR NEXT STEP IN TACTICAL ASCENT

THE ENVIRONMENT

CHANGED CONDITIONS OF COURT SURFACE and WEATHER, VENUE, etc., MUST BE REFLECTED IN TACTICS, AS MUST THE MATCH SITUATION (SCORES, SERVING OR RECEIVING, etc.)

YOUR OPPONENT

AT THE SAME TIME OPPONENT'S WEAKNESSES MUST BE EXPLOITED, ERRORS MUST BE FORCED FROM OPPONENT AND OPPONENT'S OWN TACTICS MUST BE COUNTERED AND TURNED TO ADVANTAGE

YOU

YOUR TACTICS MUST BE BASED ON YOUR OWN STRENGTHS and INITIALLY DIRECTED TOWARDS LIMITING YOUR OWN ERRORS

read
upwards

The 12 Principles of Singles Play

The end justifies the means. Tennis players will differ in the way they achieve their objectives but these principles must be borne in mind and these ends must govern your means.

Ranking The Principles

As with scientific principles, a lower ranking one cannot overturn a higher one. Although the very nature of tennis, with server and receiver alternating game by game, makes it difficult for a precise priority of relationship between two lower principles to be inescapably established, the higher principles may be definitively 'ranked' against each other. The lowest ones will always be subordinate to the very high ones, as these examples show:

(a) It would be valueless to strive for, and succeed in, recovery to a good position on court and yet fail to ensure a good return of the ball.

(b) It would not be so helpful to your cause if you made your opponent run but failed to improve your own relative court position.

(c) Hitting again to an opponent's weaker wing – probably backhand – would be inappropriate when there was a real gap for, and chance of, hitting a winner down his stronger wing – probably the forehand.

The 12 Principles of Singles

1 Put and keep the ball in play as effectively as possible.

2 Restrict your opponent's options for his next shot.

3 Put severe pressure on an opponent to create winning opportunities.

4 Take opportunities for outright winners with decisive courage.

5 Recover, or improve your own position relative to court, ball and opponent.

6 Exploit your opponent's weaknesses.

7 Make your opponent run.

8 As server utilize to the full the in-built advantage of service: as receiver use return of service to limit the server's initial superiority.

9 Ensure that the length of your shot is appropriate to the current tactical situation.

10 Play the 'percentage' shots.

11 Strive for 'STAR quality' in every one of your own shots.

12 Keep your opponent constantly guessing – and guessing wrongly – by being generally unpredictable and especially by springing sudden complete surprises.

Examine these principles closely.

1. Put and keep the ball in play as effectively as possible.

Facts

(a) If the ball does not go over the net, your efforts are in vain.

(b) If the ball fails to land in court, your net clearance is in vain.

(c) The net is lower in the middle.

(d) The diagonal route across court is longer than the straight one.

Conclusions

Height risk This must be related to your shot's speed and length.

Lowest point of the net It is easier to clear the net near its centre.

Diagonal or straight from baseline? Diagonal shots have better safety records than straight ones, except from very wide positions or when returning widely angled services.

2. Restrict your opponent's options for his next shot.

Facts

(a) An opponent has less opportunity for an outright winner from near the baseline than from near the net.

(b) An opponent cannot put away a knee-height volley as severely as he could a shoulder-height one.

(c) A balanced and controlled opponent has fewer options from near the centre of his baseline than from a position close to the tramlines.

(d) An unbalanced opponent has fewer options than a balanced one.

(e) An opponent will generally have fewer options on his weaker wing.

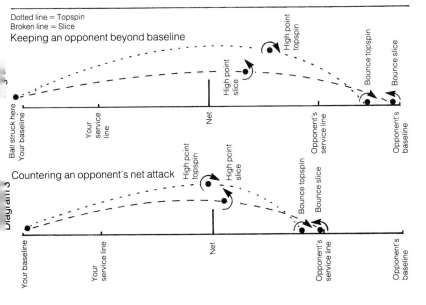

18

Conclusions

Length of Shot Length of shot is a crucial aspect of singles ground-stroke play; casual loss of length is a recipe for disaster and the golden rule of singles is to attempt to keep the opponent on or beyond his own baseline when he strikes the ball. The main exception is when playing committed baseliners who dislike the net position; they should be tempted into the forecourt under your conditions in order to expose their weak volleying.

Height of Shot When the opponent is near the net, the main aim of any shot is to get its highest point on your side of the net in order to dip it low at your opponent's feet (Diagram 3).

Angles When the 'see-saw' of any rally sees you in the high and dominant position, severe angles can be your allies, but when you are 'down and nearly out' and scrambling to escape from danger, angles can be your enemies.

Opponent's Weaker Wing Directing the ball towards an opponent's weaker wing is likely to reduce that opponent's options. However, it must be remembered that the 'weaker wing' is not necessarily the side from which the opponent hits less powerfully: some players will drive with fierce power on the forehand but erratically, whereas, though with less power, they might have great control and subtlety on the backhand. Their 'weaker wing', therefore, is the forehand side; your 'percentage shot' would, in this case, be targeted on your opponent's forehand wing.

Diagram 4a

For slice start above the ball.

Diagram 4d

For topspin start below the ball.

Stroke down the back of the ball.

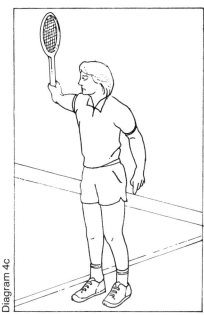

Diagram 4c

Follow through for length and control.

'Lift' the ball over the net.

Diagram 4f

Brush over ball for penetration.

3. Put severe pressure on an opponent to create winning opportunities.

Facts

(a) A high proportion of the shots coming towards you will be reasonably easy to play and return, but your own and your opponent's court positions might preclude outright winners being played.

(b) Frequently an opponent will be off balance and/or will be striving to recover his position, having been forced wide or deep in his court.

(c) At all levels, relatively few points are scored by outright winners and fewer still by sudden 'inspired' power-bolts from defensive positions. At lower standards most points accrue from unforced errors off your opponent's racket; at higher levels most come from forced errors.

Conclusions

'Easy' Shots An easier ball coming towards you should not be viewed as a welcome lull in a tough encounter; it must be positively used to press an opponent even further out of position, to stretch him wider, to unbalance him further, to tuck him up more tightly, or to hurry him into error by sheer speed and spin.

Knock Over the Unbalanced An opponent's lack of balance and position must be ruthlessly exploited to embarrass him further, to improve an attacking situation still more and even to pave the way for an outright winner.

Escalation Successful players build and maintain pressure; you should not go for the 'real hero' shots too soon.

4. Take opportunities for outright winners with decisive courage.

Facts

(a) A ball placed in an opponent's court, whether it be high or low, fast or slow, severely spun or not, long or short, or angled or straight **which the opponent cannot reach** always wins the point.

(b) Outright winners, though terminal, are rare and have to be worked for.

Conclusions

Seize Opportunities When the opportunity comes for such a winner there must be no holding back or pussy-footing around. Even the most cautious baseline-defender must be prepared to hit clinically fast and devastatingly in order to win the point, otherwise the patient build-up and earlier lesser risks will all have been in vain.

Adventure Plays Certain severely defensive situations, especially if the score is currently favourable, also demand adventurous 'going for a winner'.

Some Winners Are Not 'Heroic' A drop-shot out of reach or a sneaky, slow passing shot is just as much an outright winner as the most blasting of smashes.

5. Recover, or improve, your own position relative to court, ball and opponent.

Facts

(a) If you stand in the same place twice you are bound to be wrong.

(b) Your movement is an element that your opponent has to consider in his planning.

Conclusions

Move Every ball alters the game.

Respond Every shot played by you or your opponent and every fractional or major move by the opponent – even a slightly more intensive 'lean' into a shot, a mild sway to one side (possibly a bluff) or a greater or lesser appearance of urgency in his body's approach to the ball and the pace and pattern of his racket swing – all call for a response from you. They invariably demand a subtle, sharp or extensive alteration of your position and balance.

Improve A poor personal position relative to your own court, to the ball and to opponent must be upgraded as far as possible and a good one improved still further.

Remove If you stand still, you are removing one element from the opponent's permutations and making his calculations easier, so move even if only to deceive and then change your direction.

6. Exploit your opponent's weaknesses.

Facts

(a) Even great champions have weaknesses.

(b) It is inevitable that over time more errors will flow from an opponent's weakness than from his strength. If not, the wrong assessment of his weakness has been made.

(c) Inexperienced players will continually be seen practising forehand drives and will repeatedly fail to vary that pattern in a serious game.

(d) Unimaginative continual attention towards an opponent's weakness could prove counter-productive.

Conclusions

There Are Weaknesses Everywhere When playing a baseliner draw him in to the net. Do everything possible by way of length, spin, height of drive and pace, to deny a net-rusher any chance of coming forward over his own baseline. If you feel that you are inevitably going to hit a particular shot short, then endeavour to keep it low in its bounce – even a good net-player is more vulnerable when having to play his approach shot low and in front of him.

Backhand Usually – Forehand Occasionally At lower standards the backhand wing is almost invariably the weaker, so go ahead and attack it; but when playing against a great backhand (often a double-handed one), attack the forehand – so obvious yet so often overlooked.

Discretion Do not just plug away at a weakness, unless it is a glaring one and a treasure-house of points, but more wisely go for the weakness on a vital 30–40 or 40–30 point – or if it is a fifty-fifty choice whether to go down one wing or the other, attack the weaker.

7. Make your opponent run.

Fact

(a) **Any sensible opponent will be where he wants to be** and will be more comfortable and secure in stroke-production where he has chosen the hitting ground.

Conclusions
Where Would You Like Him? He has, therefore to be moved to where you want him to be.
Strain Produces Error Stretched and strained on the move, even a skilled ball-player will be more prone to error.

8. As server utilize to the full the built-in advantage of service: as receiver use the return of service to limit the server's initial superiority.

Facts (as Server)
(a) You have two chances of putting the ball into play.
(b) The receiver has to await your timing and intentions.
(c) The receiver will be more defensively poised and positioned when receiving your first service.
(d) The receiver will be less aggressively inclined mentally when awaiting your first service.
(e) Big first services on a slow surface rarely ace any competent receiver unless combined with accurate placement.
(f) Good serving on a fast surface usually presents good immediate net command possibilities.
(g) A double-fault is a free gift to the receiver.
(h) No service can, in purely physical terms, be hit 'flat': some spin is an inevitable consequence of the service action of all players except for very unusual giants.

Conclusions
Are You World Champion? If you serve 100% first services in to court, you are either the world champion or you could get greater penetration by risking more speed, length and spin and by sharpening the angle of delivery (Diagrams 5a/b and 6a/b).
First Service Percentages Generally about 60% to 70% really effective first services into court would be a reasonably achievable mark for most players' aspirations. Bear in mind that on a very fast surface, greater risk in striving for aces or return of service errors might be worthwhile. However, on slow to very slow surfaces wise competitors

Use of kick service in singles
With the KICK service it is the left court (ad-court) which presents right-handers the best opportunities. Exactly reversed for left-handers, it being the right-court (deuce-court) into which their KICK deliveries are most effective.

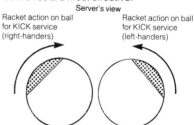

Server's view

Racket action on ball for KICK service (right-handers)

Racket action on ball for KICK service (left-handers)

Right-handers from about 8.30 to 11.30 on a clock face.

Left-handers from about 3.30 to 12.30 on a clock face.

As throw of racket head goes *forward through* ball, it should also *brush* sharply upwards and across ball to impart the impure topspin (more *brush*/KICK develops, less brush across/mild topspin results).

Use of kick service in singles to

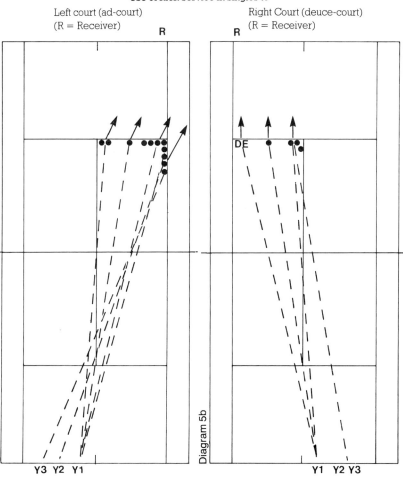

Left court (ad-court)
(R = Receiver)

Right Court (deuce-court)
(R = Receiver)

R

R

DE

Diagram 5b

Y3 Y2 Y1

Y1 Y2 Y3

Y1 = Usual position you should
     adopt when serving
Y2 = Frequent position for
     more severe angle
Y3 = Occasional surprise
     position

Y1 = Usual position you should
     adopt when serving
Y2 = Possible change of angle
     position
Y3 = Occasional surprise
     position
DE = Difficult but effective

Above and below: Brush up for KICK.

Above and below: Drag down for SLICE.

Take all the time you need over first and especially second service. Never be rushed into a fault, or double-fault.

When close to the net keep your racket high and ready for decisive action, as demonstrated by Jimmy Arias.

Use of slice service in singles to

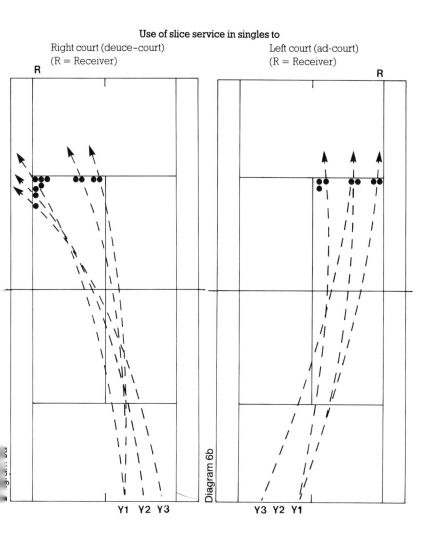

Right court (deuce–court)
(R = Receiver)

Left court (ad–court)
(R = Receiver)

Diagram 6b

Y1 Y2 Y3

Y3 Y2 Y1

Y1 = Usual position you should
 adopt when serving
Y2 = Occasional position for
 more severe angle
Y3 = Very occasional surprise
 position

Y1 = Usual position you should
 adopt when serving
Y2 _ Occasional positions
Y3 = for variation of angle

Use of slice service in singles
The right court (deuce-court) presents right-handers with greater SLICE opportunities, it being exactly reversed for left-handers with the left court (ad-court) being their SLICE harvest-field!

Server's view

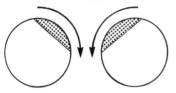

Racket action on ball for SLICE service (right-handers)   Racket action on ball for SLICE service (left-handers)

Right-handers from about 12.30 to 2.30 on a clock face   Left-handers from about 11.30 to 9.30 on a clock face

As throw of racket head goes *forward through* ball, it should also *brush* sharply downwards and around ball to impart the SLICE (more *brush*/more slice, more *through*/milder slice).

aim for even sounder first service security.

The Driving Seat You will certainly be in this seat more often when you commence the point with a fairly good first service as compared with a pretty hot second ball.

Composure You should take your time and gather composure and balance before delivering either the first or second services.

Plan and Aim You should have a plan and target for every service. Do not just aim for the service-court unless you are virtually a beginner.

Exorbitant Double Faults A double fault is a price no player can afford on a game point either way.

Very Expensive Double Faults A double fault is a price an inexperienced player cannot afford on any point.

Expensive Double Faults A double fault is the price an experienced player must occasionally pay in order to maintain offensive pressure via the second service ball, especially on faster surfaces.

Service 'Charge' Preparation If you have ambitions to be an all-out attacking and dominating volleyer at the net, you will do well to pay as much, if not more, attention to your service preparation, intentions and actions and to your approach run, as you pay to your volleying technique.

Facts (as Receiver)
(a) The service has to be delivered to a restricted part of the whole court.

(b) If you are wrongly placed to receive an early first service in a match and do not adjust, you could be ineffectually placed throughout the encounter.

(c) It will be a very unusual server who is more aggressive on second service than on first.

(d) A receiver positioned nearer the net limits angle of service, restricts server's recovery time and has more return options.

(e) A receiver positioned farther from the net has more time to deal with sheer speed of service or with severe spins, but has fewer return options.

(f) The score will condition a server's thinking and action.

(g) The server is more vulnerable after a second service than after a first.

(h) A receiver is more likely to win

the point if the return is deep when the server stays back, or if the return is low when the server follows service in to the net.

(i) Returning fierce first serving could be considered successful if it limits the server's choices and evens up the winning/losing balance on that rally merely to 50–50; whilst return of average second serving could only be considered successful if it improved receiver's chances to about 70–30.

Conclusions
Position Return of service is the most vital shot the receiver plays and the basic position for it should not be unthinkingly taken up. Such a position must be continually monitored for suitability relative to the server's deliveries, the surface and the weather conditions.

Blocking Against thunderous attacking serving, a receiver might well have to be content with merely blocking the ball back securely into court on some occasions, especially on game points.

Move in Against Second Services As receiver you should move in early (partially even before the server serves) to attack second services, especially when the score is in your favour.

Backhand Return Vulnerability By its very nature, service from the right court leaves a right-hander's backhand vulnerable deep in the court and vice-versa for left-handers in serving from the left court.

Length and Height As in general play, the main aims of the receiver are depth of return (long) when the server stays back and height of return (low) when the server rushes to the net (Diagrams 2, 3, 4a-f, 7a/b).

Variety Imaginative variety of pace, spin and angle, in returning service will help to reduce the server's initial advantage.

Spin Topspin and slice are very important weapons in a receiver's armoury.

9. Ensure that the length of your shot is appropriate to the tactical situation.

Facts
(a) A short shot from you frequently provides an opportunity for your opponent to command the net.

(b) A drive from you aimed long but not successful in passing your opponent will normally give him an easy volleying opportunity.

(c) A severely fast but straight hit volley bouncing mid-court could well prove to be an easy ball for your opponent to collect and return from his own baseline.

(d) It is when, where and how the opponent has to cope with your shot which is vital rather than where you actually make your shot pitch.

Conclusions
Trajectory The length and height of your shot's trajectory must be appropriate to the tactic upon which you have decided – ie appropriate to the desired result of your shot.

'Good' Length A 'good' length, therefore, is not always a 'great' length.

Duration of flight Some shots need to reach the opponent quickly, others more slowly.

28

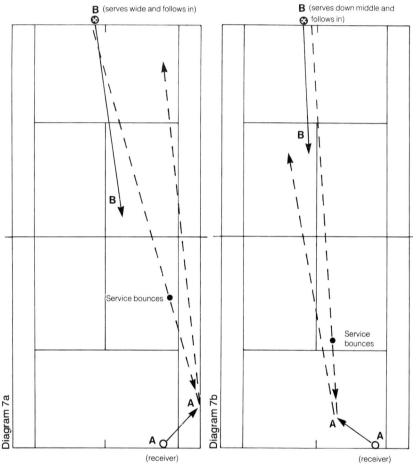

Receiver's percentage target areas (Right court. Similar in reverse for left court.)

Diagram 7a

Diagram 7b

You are A (receiver) and your percentage shot to a wide service is the down-the-line ball. If server stays near his baseline this is still your percentage return.

When server aims down the middle, receiver's best answer is back down the middle against incoming server. If server stays near his baseline, aim for his backhand.

10. Play the 'percentage' shots.

Fact

In every situation there will be shots which have a high success rate and those which, although effective in other conditions, have too high a risk element to consider relative to the ball to be played, to your position, to your opponent's position and to the score.

Conclusions

'Rose-tinted Spectacles' Although a hair-raising shot coming off delights you and any spectators and is re-membered clearly and proudly, achieving it might well have cost two or three errors when it did not come off.

'Percentage Winners' When Losing Any time when you are game-point down you should most definitely play the percentage shot, unless you are already on the ATP/WTA computers. That way you just might join those exalted beings one day.

11. Strive for 'STAR quality' in every one of your own shots.

Facts

(a) A shot has these elements to be balanced and exploited:

Speed
Trajectory
Aiming-point
Rotation

(b) It has not so far proved possible for a human being to hit a tennis ball without imparting spin.

(c) Certain tactical situations will demand excessive spin: other situa-

tions will require the very minimum of spin.

(d) Spin will affect a ball's length and penetration (Diagrams 2, 3 and 4).

(e) A ball may be hit to travel long/short, high/low, fast/slowly and straight/angled in relation to the court.

Conclusions

Blend An attempt must be made to balance these four elements to greatest tactical effect in each and every shot played.

Examples Examples of the myriad permutations are:

(i) A slow highish sliced straight drive suitable for a backhand approach shot leading to net command.

(ii) A low fast heavy topspin angled drive suitable for crossing and passing a volleyer at the net.

(iii) A medium-paced heavily chopped low long straight volley suitable for keeping a net player out of real trouble.

(iv) A fast flattish short angled volley killing a high ball at the net.

Vital Differences Make a Vital Difference The selection and nature of these ingredients is yours to command and will depend upon what your opponent has done to you and what you wish to do to him, but the correct choices over the whole match could alone represent the difference between a 5–7, 5–7 loss and a 6–0, 6–0 win between players who look to be evenly matched.

12. Keep your opponent constantly guessing – and guessing wrongly – by being unpredictable and by springing complete surprises.

Facts
(a) Your opponent will largely see what he expects to see.
(b) A long encounter (point/game/set/match/series of matches against the same opponent) will establish its own pattern and predictability.

Conclusions
Surprise Success will result from effective unpredictability.

Examples Wrong-footing a player by placing the ball almost exactly back where he has just come from is the most common example of a surprise move (if a 'surprise' tactic can be common). Other examples are:
(i) Serving a comparatively slow first service.
(ii) When at least two points clear suddenly present your opponent with an easy ball on his strength.
(iii) Drive straight at an opponent, perhaps off one of his smashes.
Trump Cards Save your best surprises for set points.

Your Effectiveness as a Singles Player

Objectives
Remember that the objectives of singles play are:
1. To limit your own errors.
2. To force errors from your opponent.

Many unforced errors are caused by faulty technique and seeking out a coach or studying a book directly concerned with technique would be advisable (see Appendix).

However, even without *conscious* technical change on your part, you will reduce your own errors and gradually increase pressure on your opponent if you can achieve more effective on-court practice, positioning and decision making.

Much improvement takes place *unconsciously* and imperceptibly. You do not have to be taught or coached in order to learn.

The Importance of Practice
Enjoyable, active, functional practice is vital in achieving positive change and increased total on-court effectiveness. Learning is a sustained change in the way in which you perform a certain task. Be warned that you can actually learn to perform a task less effectively.

Realistic practice and conditioned games – simulated match-play with an extra rule putting emphasis on developing particular aspects of play – is a pleasant way of inducing positive change in your tennis responses.

If you link practice, study of this book and watching and competing against better players, you will widen your tactical arsenal and be quicker and more accurate in selecting the right tactical weapons.

On-court Practice

So, go on court with a like-minded player and try these practices, remembering that for both of you to benefit fully there must be:

* An element of co-operation.
* An element of competition.
* Total concentration.
* Regular change of emphasis and role to prevent you getting stale.
* A good supply of balls to save time.
* An intensive fixed time period – not vague and desultory play.
* An *objective* in the minds of both players.

Enjoyable Functional Practices

1. Limiting Error

Attempt a rally of just five consecutive, good length, hard-hit shots (Diagram 8). After achieving five, try to make it six in your next rally, and so on. When you fail to reach a target, revert to five and start the process again. Use the whole court, the half-court straight, or the half-court diagonally as shown in the diagram.

2. Co-operate – then Compete

Play 21 points as in table tennis, commencing with a service or a plain underarm drive to feed the ball into play as appropriate. *Co-operate* until five shots have been played: then *compete* for the point in the normal way, scoring as one to the winner.

A player making an *unforced* error in the first five co-operating shots deducts two points from any score that he has. Sensible play within the spirit of this practice

Co-operating on drives

Use one long half of the doubles court as below. Aim to put ball well up to baseline.

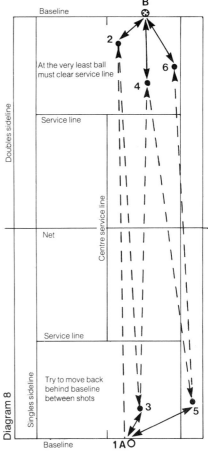

You, as A, commence and both you and practice partner B try to hit with controlled power and placement. Also use other half and progress to diagonal halves and to whole of singles court.

should eliminate most errors up to five drives, whilst craftily setting up positions for the competitive phase.

3. Backhand Emphasis

Play as for Practice 2 above, but in the five shot co-operating phase count only backhand drives. Any shot may be played but only backhand drives count towards the qualifying five.

This type of practice particularly encourages less experienced tacticians to seek out a likely weakness of an opponent at the same time as gradually trying to eliminate unforced errors on one's own backhand drive.

4. Attack and Defence

Take turns at being attacker and defender. The attacker has to take the defender's five *lives* as quickly as possible because defender is counting every time he strikes the ball. Defender also gets a bonus of ten every time attacker fails to win a rally.

For example, the defender might return four shots into court before losing first rally, then eight shots before succumbing in second rally. Defender's score is now 12. On the next rally the defender returns ball into court three times and also wins rally for a ten bonus – score is now 25 and so on.

When the attacker has taken all five lives, he becomes defender and tries to score more points for his five lives. There is a good balance here between adventurous attacking pressure and steady delaying defence.

5. Stroke Emphasis

Play as for Practice 4 but with the defender only counting his hits on a particular stroke – forehand or backhand drive. This opens up two new tactical aspects. The attacker will not merely plug away at a weakish backhand if he is giving the defender a point every time the defender hits it, but will switch decisively to that backhand wing having created space and opportunity. In return the defender will have to tighten up on his weaker wing or seek ways of earlier positioning to make more forcing shots from his stronger wing.

6. Mats Win Matches

A practice favoured by top players is to put old car mats down on court (Diagrams 9a/b) and rally firmly and strongly, aiming for them.

Such targets will usually be placed near corners but do not make the task disheartening by placing tiny beer mats right at the extreme edges of the court.

Hoops, boxes and, on some courts, chalked areas, may be used but mats are safe and convenient and make good targets, especially if there is a strong colour contrast with the court's surface. The consistency and length, vital to successful singles play, will be encouraged and severity of shot will develop if you hit for the mat and do not just 'drop' the ball on it.

Why Tactics Drills?

You may now be saying to yourself, 'I wanted tactical advice – a few tricks to beat players X and Y and become club champion – not details

Mats could help you win matches

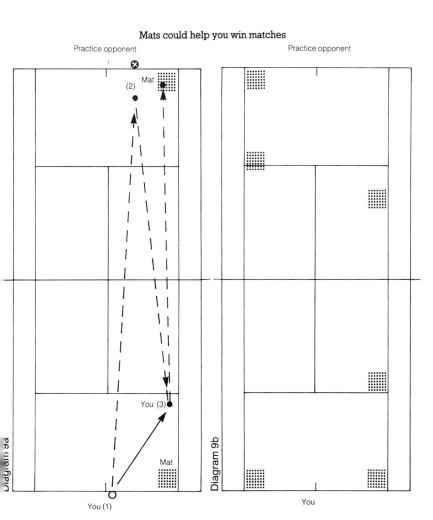

You manage to hit target with third shot of this rally.

Vary your practice by varying target positions.

of drills however enjoyable they may be.' By way of reply consider the following three paragraphs carefully.

Davis (or Federation) Cup Conversation

When on TV you see a Team Captain whispering into a star tennis player's ear during a vital Davis Cup (or other) match, probably a very basic point is being emphasized. 'Hang in there – your opponent is on a real high at the moment but you are doing all the right things and playing the shots likely to beat him; he'll blow soon – just keep at him and keep your errors down.' The advice is likely to be simple and encouraging and might be no more than, 'Watch the ball more closely' – or – 'Move those feet for better position around the ball.'

Half Or Full Story

Just *talking tactics*, absorbing them into your mind and thinking big and positively is an important half of the story; but it is only half the story. You have to go out there and make the ideas work, normally at a tempo not of your choosing.

A famous general (Moltke) said that the best training for war was war itself and McEnroe and Fleming prepared for many great doubles victories by playing singles (or diagonal half court doubles) beforehand. Seek out match-play whenever possible, trying out your less familiar and more imaginative tactics against weaker opposition. You should also seek out intelligent players prepared *to work at their play.*

Inexperienced Competitors

Inexperienced competitors tend to do four things on court:
* Win.
* Lose.
* Hope that three inspired minutes hitting before the match starts will

rectify years of neglect.
* Practise big forehands to the exclusion of all else.

Move out of the ranks of unthinking hitters of a tennis ball. Do what most of 'The Young Masters' do in their practice time – simulate match conditions but without the match pressures and time consuming rituals.

The first six practices suggested were aimed at limiting your errors, with a gradual escalation of pressure on your opponent by hitting to definite areas and restricting opponent's options.

Now challenge yourself to hurry and harry an opponent via these next four practices.

7. Pressing To Win

Play an ordinary point. Whoever wins it has to win the next point inside ten shots (five each). If successful again, then next point must be won inside nine shots and so on. If the other player merely survives the required number of shots in any rally, he takes over as pressing player trying to win inside ten, then nine, etc. Squeezing an opponent down to three shots not only makes you think very seriously about placing that first ball but is the equivalent of putting two games safely under your belt in a match – and two consecutive games at any score is a strategical gain to be treasured.

Good destructive placement is encouraged by practising like this over the whole court and penetrative pace is developed by the half-court practice. When looking for a quick winner in the half-court practice remember stop volley, drop-shot and lob, separately or combined in a sequence. Less experienced players, taking turns at feeding first ball, will begin to think more positively about placing that first drive but stronger players should always make the pressing player serve and thus focus on aggressive first serving.

Effective Practice
Even if you have been only partially successful in making these practices work on court you have given on-court attention to the first three principles of singles tactics and to the sixth. The next three practices highlight the vital fourth, fifth and seventh principles:
★ Making winners.
★ Good personal positioning.
★ Moving your opponent about the court.

8. Running Drives
You are attempting to retain a good position near the centre of your baseline whilst returning the ball consistently to one side of your opponent's court. Your opponent is trying to 'spread' you about the court making you play sharply angled forehands and straight backhands (Diagram 10). Take turns in both roles and in basing the practice on left half of court. Develop to both players being 'Running Drivers' (Diagram 11).

Your movements then are realistically close to baseline rallying in a match and you are improving speed about the court, suppleness and strength on the turn, and stamina, all crucial to implementing your tactics.

Running drives (basic)
B is attempting to limit own error whilst moving A severely from side to side.

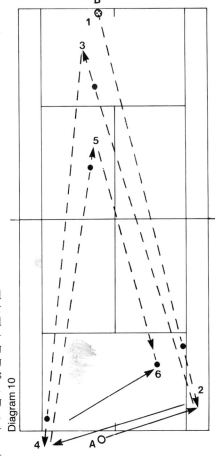

You are A (the running driver) always aiming to return ball strongly to one half of B's court.

Running drives (both)
Develop this with both A and B being running drivers.

Running drives (after service)
B is receiver and on this occasion is always aiming ball for right half of A's court.

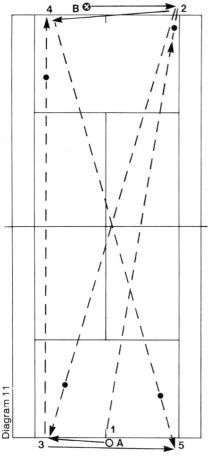

Co-operate early on, then *compete*.

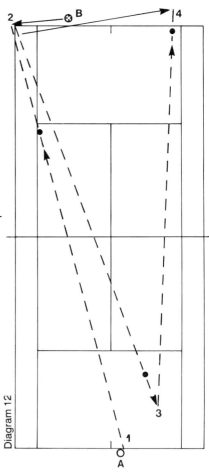

9. Conditioned Games
Study diagrams 12–15 and set up the different serving, receiving and follow-on situations.

As A, you are serving severely wide to set up an attack on B's backhand, intending to keep him scampering!

Running drives
Receiver B attacks server's backhand after wide service.

Running drives
Practise similar situations with running drives for server and/or receiver following service down the middle, etc.

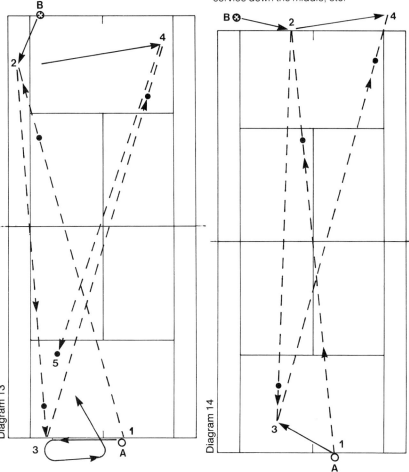

Diagram 13

Diagram 14

If a wide service is not severe enough, you as server (A) might have to survive a backhand pounding and incur as much running as B.

Note how server A's delivery down middle limits receiver B's angles of return.

Running drives
Particularly practise all angles of service and return in the vital left (ad-court).

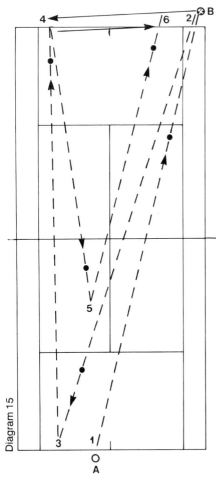

Diagram 15

Server A could attack a possible backhand weakness of receiver B and set B off on the 'running-treadmill' again until B drops one short enough for A to kill.

10. Make Your Service Count
Serve and go in to the net, or serve and look for opportunities to get to the net fairly quickly. If you win the point from the baseline you serve again but with only one service. If, however, you win the point commanding the net, or genuinely en route there, you have two services again.

As soon as you lose a point your practice opponent serves and the eventual winner is the one who strings together the longest sequence of winning points. Crisp serving is required to set up good volleying chances and opportunities to get to the net must not be wasted. Especially, do not overlook the occasional wrong-footing volley back to where you angled a service, whilst the opponent is scampering to cover an exposed gap.

This type of practice sharpens thoughts on placement of service and your positioning in play.

Positioning
Basic positions for the server or as the receiver are illustrated in Diagram 16, with the main variations included as appropriate to standard and conditions.

Shading
As the rally develops positioning is regularly a case of 'shading', as the top players call it, to cover the likely angles of return. Study diagrams 17–20 and note how on the baseline you generally shade away from the ball's position in the opponent's court and yet when approaching the net you usually shade towards the ball.

Basic positions and No Man's Land
Receiver B usually stands as marked. Edge to B(W) if backhand weak. Ease back (to B1) on fast services. Press forward on slow deliveries to B2.

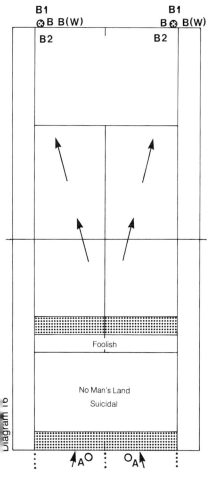

Diagram 16

Service, usually from A, may be from anywhere behind baseline, within dotted lines. Avoid No Man's Land during play.

Baseline Positioning
This involves begrudging every inch that you are moved away from a central point, covering all likely angles, except when running confidently across to crash home an outright winner. Obviously, if you are really making a winner, recovery of your position is unimportant.

Balanced, immediate return to your best 'shading' position, as illustrated, should be your immediate concern after each shot – hit and move. Sometimes your movement might involve edging in to No Man's Land (Diagram 16) when you have really stretched your opponent and anticipate a weakish return. You should also have the courage to move positively into No Man's Land to limit the return angles (Diagram 21) after playing a drop-shot, wittingly or unwittingly.

Approaching And Commanding The Net
In singles you should follow the line of the ball as you approach the net (Diagrams 19, 20). You will have a better chance of success at the net if your approach shot forces your opponent to make contact with the ball outside the court lines (Diags.19, 20).

Objectives Of Approach Shots
These should be to bring your strengths to bear on your opponent's weakness and to compel your opponent to make hurried contact with the ball beyond his baseline – beyond a sideline *as well* would be a bonus. Rarely approach on severely angled shots unless the opponent is very hard pressed by

In-play positioning (staying back on baseline)

Once in play all your positioning must be in relation to the ball. If you hit to an angle and stay back, do *not* cover the exact centre of your baseline but 'shade' appropriately as shown below.

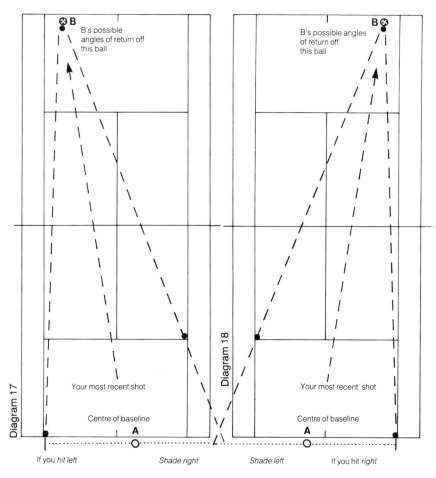

As A you position yourself broadly in the centre of the dotted lines to cover B's likely angles of return most effectively.

In-play positioning (approaching the net)

The diagrams show how making opponent B play the ball outside his court lines gives you, as A, better chances of covering B's likely angles of return.

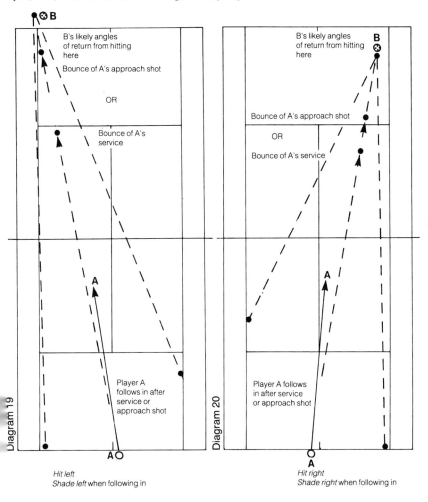

Hit left
Shade left when following in

Hit right
Shade right when following in

Exactly the opposite of 'shading' applies when approaching the net. You should shade towards the side *to which you have hit the ball.*

42

Drop-shot action and reaction
B is at B1 when A drop-shots him; he moves to B2 to counter it. Off a good drop-shot B's percentage shot is straight down the sideline.

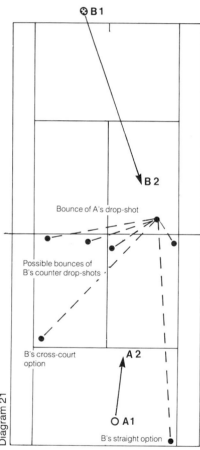

Bounce of A's drop-shot

Possible bounces of B's counter drop-shots

B's cross-court option

A 2

O A1

B's straight option

Diagram 21

Having played a drop-shot from area of A1, A would be wise to edge further into No Man's Land to A2 in order to cover B's possible return angles or any counter drop-shots from B.

them (Diagram 19). On fast surfaces most players should strive for command of the net after service and there will be times when even committed baseliners must steal in there to knock-out a rather surprised opponent.

Executing Approach Shots
Do not let the ball drop too low and try to take it alongside the body allowing you *to carry* the approach drive with you as part of a balanced run-in. Remember that you are often in mid-court and that the ball must be sent off on a shorter journey with a lower trajectory. Do not half wish for a winner but hit approach shots securely, safely clear of the net and inside the lines.

The Next Step
If you thoroughly explore the twelve principles of singles via these practices, you are ready to put into on-court effect these guidelines for the roles you will have to play as a singles competitor.

SINGLES ROLES
First, what are the main singles roles which you might want to play and which you might have to play?
* Fighting it out from the baseline.
* Baselining against net attack.
* Striving for net command as server.
* Striving for net command as receiver.
* Striving for net command after rallying.
* Mixing it.
* Playing as a left-hander.
* Playing as a two-hander.

Why straight is the percentage option
(When B is approaching net or has been pulled to net by A's drop-shot.)

If B plays his shot at B1 it is obviously more hazardous moving to covering position B2 off angled approach. The percentage shot is straight making B1/B2 move easy.

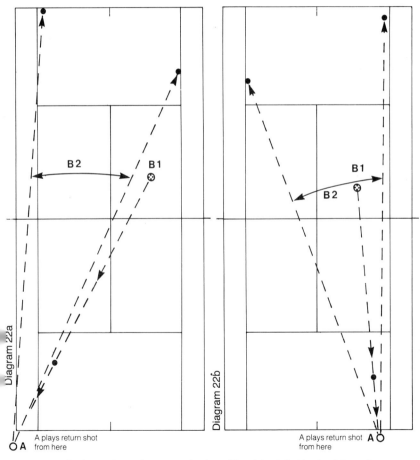

Diagram 22a

Diagram 22b

A plays return shot from here

A plays return shot from here

It will naturally depend greatly on exactly where B's original shot is struck from, its severity of spin and pace and A's recovery position and balance, but if B's ANGLED approach does not come off, A should have a 'field day' – the field is so wide! Be sure to remember this advice when you are next at B1!

FIGHTING IT OUT FROM THE BASELINE
Upset Opponent's Rhythm and Pace
Endlessly vary the direction, spin, speed and height of your shots. Be generally unpredictable.

Limit Angles
Keep in mind the maxim 'change the angle and lose the point'. You can vary the *direction* of your shot without switching right across court to the other angle: only change the *angle* if you are under pressure and just cannot play it anywhere else, or if you see it as a chance to push the 'rally see-saw' upwards in your favour. Do not change because you are getting bored – look at two star players slugging it out and note how only positive angle change takes place (Diagram 23).

Be very wary of the straight down the line shot which you might attempt to play in answer to an opponent's cross-court drive. Look at Diagram 23 and keep firmly in mind the warning that this is one of the riskiest drives a baseliner can play if it is taken close to the junction of his own baseline and sideline.

Be Alert For Another 'Backhand' Danger
Move really fast in recovering your basic central position if you have been pulled to your forehand and slightly forward and if you anticipate that the next ball which you might have to play could be long to your backhand. If this scenario does develop it could see you having to play a ball behind the 'running-line of your body'.

Offensive changing of angles
It is assumed that player B generally has good control and penetration on drives.

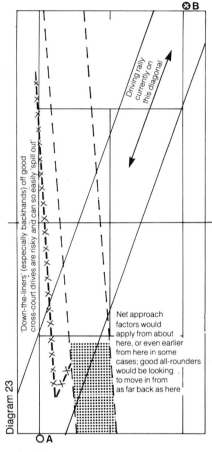

Attacking change of angle is best considered by you (A) if you are able to make contact with B's drive within the shaded area. Crosses indicate slim error margin when going straight off a deep cross-court ball.

On the backhand especially, contact of racket and ball even slightly farther from the net than the most advanced point of your body causes problems. It greatly reduces your options and almost invariably means that any drive you execute has to be down the line or to the centre of the court – the cross-court option is virtually non-existent and your opponent might know this (Diagram 24).

Exploiting Angles

Use this same tactic of first hitting wide and slightly short to your opponent's forehand and then deep to his backhand, knowing that, if you are successful, your opponent is restricted to a smallish target area on your forehand. This could result in your being able to make an outright winner, or at worst a real 'opponent's-thigh-stretcher' to his forehand. Alternatively that deep ball to behind his running body on his backhand might provide a chance for one of those stealthy tiptoe net approaches which even the most committed of baseliners should have tucked up their tactical sleeves.

Understand that, because of the risks involved, *severe* angles should be thought of as winning shots – *outright winners*. Avoid playing too many geometrical impossibilities intended as softening up shots.

Drop-shots

Do not neglect the use of the drop-shot. Save it for occasions when you are placed right inside your own No Man's Land and when your opponent is well back on his own

Opponent chasing after a backhand
Opponent B running back to play a backhand behind the line of his body is almost certain to present a good volley opportunity for A.

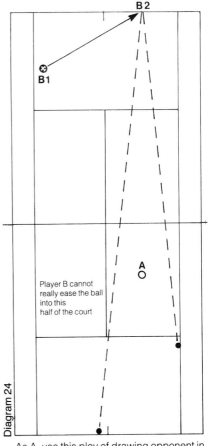

Diagram 24

B2

B1

A

Player B cannot really ease the ball into this half of the court

As A, use this ploy of drawing opponent in on forehand then hitting long to backhand, but be alert to a possible lob from B. Also, beware of being caught in this 'running backwards for a backhand' trap yourself.

baseline. Pick as your target the area diagonally farthest from his position, unless you are intending to wrong foot him. Aim the ball to fall like a snowflake down his side of the net (Diagram 21) and edge even nearer the net yourself. This will see you poised to pick up any countering drop-shot from your opponent and to bisect more securely his possible angles of driving shots.

Drop-shots should really be intended outright winners each time, but you and he would not be baselining it if you felt as confident and competent at net play. Therefore, just drawing him, hurried and unbalanced to the net area, could be to your distinct advantage, as it would be a case of your rear court strength against his front court weakness.

Your Strengths Versus His Weaknesses

Your objective is to keep your strengths bearing on your opponent's weaknesses. Not quite to the exclusion of all else as unimaginative play to an opponent's weakness could well 'play that shot in', or you might be so predictable that an opponent was forewarned and ready to run around a weak backhand. However, it could certainly mean that you took most opportunities to run around your own backhand and fire off a devastating forehand instead. It could also mean lack of interest and variety in a match. It is worth mentioning three points here:

1. Your primary objective on court is to win – not to entertain. If the manner of your win is pleasing to you, that's a bonus; if the manner of your win is pleasing to you *and* to the spectators, that's a double bonus.

2. If you have a really good forehand and a weakish backhand, you are a good tactician and move well if you play only one in ten shots on your backhand. However, if in such a match, you play more backhands than forehands you are a poor mover, a poor tactician or playing a masterly thinker, or all three. You might still win but not by the right margin.

3. Matches of any significance are not vehicles for exercising your weaknesses. Experiment only in practice matches or against very low-level opposition, escalating gradually. Weaknesses should be hidden, not paraded, so watch where you stand receiving service – is it more or less a placard announcing, 'I have no backhand?'

Determination In Termination

Situations will occur when even committed safety-first baseliners will be forced to the net or will have opportunities for good command of the net, which must be taken. Think about it – presumably your volleying and close to net ground strokes are not as good as your long play or you would not be a baseliner. Make your one golden volley opportunity cost-effective as a winner. Your clever stone-walling set up this chance but do not play safe at the net and risk it all on possible further volleys.

BASELINING AGAINST NET ATTACK

The golden rule is to play passing-shots or limiting shots calmly and fully. Avoid hurried snatches – keep your head steady, your eyes on the ball and no quick looking up to see if the ball is on target. Complete the job of stroking the ball fully first, then observe and recover. This advice is particularly important if your opponent is already at the net. If he is camped there, take all the time you have – precision of return in such situations is more valuable than haste.

Positioning

Between shots position yourself relative to the *direction* in which you have played your previous stroke (Diagrams 17, 18).

Beware of being too far back behind the baseline on a fast court. Pace and angle will defeat you if you allow them to on fast surfaces, so you *might* have to take an earlier ball on a faster surface.

The exception is on return of service position on any court. The question you ask yourself here is: 'Is the opponent getting as far in to the net as he wishes to before I can make him hit my return?' If the answer is yes, then take even more prolonged care over your return by perhaps standing a foot or two farther *back* to receive the first service. If it is no, then take a risk, pick up the rising ball off his service and rush him into error by hurrying the ball back to him and catching him low at his feet while he is en route to the net.

Directing Returns

If you are having to receive many good first services down the middle, be content to place your returns back to the middle of the court as low as possible, especially if you are on a fast surface (Diagrams 7a/b). When a severe first service swings you wide, your best regular return is down the line (Diagrams 7a/b). If an opponent serves a second ball on a slow surface and still comes in behind it (and is *not* an international star) then just take your time and place that ball into either gap left or right of him.

Taking your time here means not going for the hero-shot. Instead, go for direction (precise) and height (low) but still try to take the ball well inside your baseline (Diagrams 7a/b).

Soften Him Up First

Although the server is usually most vulnerable en route to the net, ie on the shot you have to play in return of his service or in reply to his approach drive, do not feel that you always have to pass the opponent outright. A well directed shot can draw an opponent into a weakish volley on one side, exposing the other wing for a more explosive shot from you to find a winning gap (Diagram 25).

Raise Your Sights

Do not neglect the last ditch defensive lob. If you find yourself way out of court, or desperately unbalanced – buy time (Diagram 26). Also most definitely do not neglect the attacking lob and remember that any lob

Manipulate then annihilate

Do not always go for the first time outright passing shot, especially if B is a timid volleyer or far from net.

Lobbing target areas

If B is a right-hander aim for BR; if B is a left-hander aim for BL.

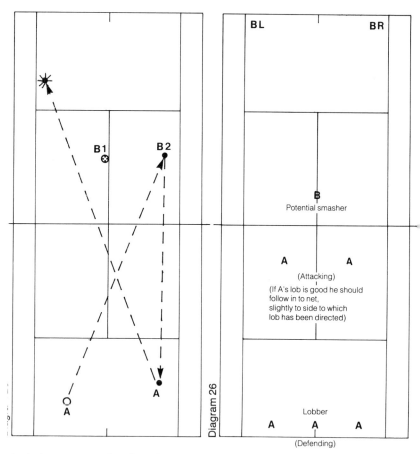

As A, draw opponent from B1 to B2 with a 'slithery dink shot' or fierce topspin angle, then hit a winner to the unguarded side.

If A's lob is poor he should quickly retreat behind baseline (centrally or slightly away from direction of lob). If pulled to the side and in doubt, lob diagonally.

Look smart and confident at the start of a match even if you do need support for shaking knees.

If your tactical decision is to go for a winner do not hold back. Commit yourself fully as Ivan Lendl does here.

is usually more effective if aimed over the opponent's non-racket shoulder (left shoulder for right-handers and vice versa).

Unless you are already top county class, be aware when lobbing that, although length is extremely important in a lob, *height* is crucial – inexperienced opponents will not relish smashing *very high* balls dropping on or just behind the service line, so save a defensive situation with height first and length second.

STRIVING FOR NET COMMAND AS SERVER
Approaching The Net Directly From Service
Essential ingredients of successful tactics are planning, movement and co-ordination. As server trying to command the net, you should co-ordinate three definite intentions – your service intention, movement intention and shot intention.

Service Intention
Have a definite target area for each service, using the maximum pace compatible with your playing standard and with a determination to put 60%–70% of first services into court. Your chances of winning the point off good first services, well followed up with swift net attack, are twice those off second services.

Movement Intention
Note how the server in photos 1–4 has merged the end of the service action with the first stride of his run-in. By the time even a fast service bounces you should be more than a

third of the way in (Diagram 27) and your first volley should be made from well inside your service court.

Do not run blindly for the centre of the net. Approach fast but be balanced and ready for action, 'shading' towards the line of your service-ball.

Avoid sudden directional changes by studying receiver's return intentions.

Shot Intention
If your opponent's return is high enough put it away firmly. If it is awkwardly low and wide, 'place' your return, often going for the security of the middle lower net which also limits the receiver's angles. Tall players should really crowd in to the net because it is the low volleys, especially cross-court ones, which are the more difficult for them. The nippy, agile, shorter player deals with these well, but finds the higher down the line stretches more difficult and, of course, must always be alert for lobs. Remember that a smooth half-volley is usually preferable to a hurried half-drive, that a low volley is better than a half-volley and that a high volley is the real prize, so keep moving in.

Building Up To Net Command
On slower surfaces at lower standards, the server should avoid charging in after a weakish service. However, even in this situation the server should be in the driving seat for *eventual* net command. When you *feel* that you have hit a good service, especially one of good pace and angle, do not merely stay where you have served or automatically

Following in after service
B is receiver facing a slice service nudging in to his body.

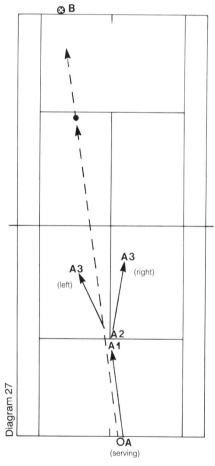

Diagram 27

A should try to reach A1 by the time service bounces and A2 by time opponent hits the ball. Move even further in to meet volley at A3 left or right.

Following in after service
Study the court plan on the left and the photographs on the opposite page.

In the left court (photo 1) and right court (photos 2 and 3) server must position himself near the centre mark and must take time over a calm and deliberate build up.

He must use his reach and power in throwing racket head at the ball, merging final leg movement of service action into an urgent run towards net (photos 2 and 3).

How far server gets along the 'run-in-trail' before receiver hits the ball will depend upon speed and angle of service and server's physique and fitness, but he should strive to be somewhere near A1 and A2, reading opponent's 'signals' all the time to discover likely line of return ball as early as possible.

Try to be set and balanced for the volley, or, if more experienced, volley with secure racket-face control (photo 4) as part of a confident surge into total net domination.

return behind the centre of your baseline. Edge in towards the ball, half expecting a shortish return. Make room for your shot by moving your feet briskly, and 'press' that ball away as far as possible from your opponent, moving immediately to the net as part of your follow-through.

Remember, it is always safer to go to the net behind a down the line or a middle of court shot, rather than a cross-court one. Remember also, that almost certainly an approach shot from well inside your own court will require slice or topspin.

STRIVING FOR NET COMMAND AS RECEIVER
Against First Service
In middle standard play – club singles or weakish early rounds of a rural county singles championship – many players will serve really good first balls but then not dream of going in behind them to the net. They are wasting the risk they have taken on that service, so, as receiver, 'ride with the surge of power' on this kind of service by getting it back safely and deep. Use the sheer pace of the service itself to aid your return, but do not flail wildly, hoping for an ace return placement off what was very nearly an ace service placement.

Often, after the effort of such service, the server (especially a tall, heavy-moving one) will be exceptionally vulnerable to your good length return. Your best opportunity for an approach shot could come from the server's very first hurriedly produced drive.

Against Second Service
Edge in anyway ready to attack a second service and go for firm solid placement. Try to categorize your opponent's second services very early as:
★ Those which are tough and could lose you the point unless you take care.
★ Those which are ripe for your attacking approach shots.
★ Those which are just asking to be hit for outright winners.

Weaker players tend to confuse the last two categories and fall between the two aims. Your 'intended winner' may legitimately have extreme pace and angle, be very low over the net and bounce near the outer lines, with all the inherent risks of such a shot. Your intended approach should pressurize but not necessarily penetrate and should be safely above net height and inside the lines.

Be confident; the odds are in the receiver's favour when a server comes in behind a second service, unless you happen to be playing someone with a viciously high-kicking second service or someone way above you in standard.

After Rallying With Server
You are waiting for a short one, so the objective of your rally is to get a short one. Varying your pace will be a way of encouraging an opponent to provide you with a short ball. Working patiently but positively in the course of a 'slugfest' (a heavy battering 'festival' of ball after ball being slammed back and forth often on the same diagonal angle) for the inevitable short ball is another possibility.

Be balanced ready for the short ball. Do not try to go in behind a ball which you have struck from well behind the baseline. Even good volleyers cannot cover the ground to gain a sound net position when the opponent has such time and space to play a passing shot.

Wait for the short ball and consider taking it early by using a sliced drive. This gives early lift to the ball for safe net clearance, then keeps the ball low on the bounce, often forcing up an easier volley for you.

MIXING IT
All-rounders

Some players will enjoy trying every facet of the game; others will either naturally, or by careful nurturing, have become all-round players, as happy at the net as on the baseline. When they are successful they will be *really* successful such as a Navratilova or an Ashe. More common will be players good enough and versatile enough to vary their game to maximum effect against a particular opponent or to make maximum use of a slow or a fast surface.

Changing A Losing Game

'Mixing it' might also be appropriate for the most committed of baseline-hugging specialists, or net-hogging crusaders. If such players find themselves 6–0, 3–0 and 30-Love down, having stuck firmly to their specialist game, they might as well try something different, don't you think?

Surface Mixer

A 'mixer' could be a singles player who, on fast surfaces, always goes in to the net *behind his own first service*. He also tries to gain a net position quickly off his opponent's second service, but is prepared to 'graft' patiently for opportunities of net command off his own second service, and will competently baseline it against any net attacks off his opponent's first service.

'Mixing it' could mean that a player will sensibly strive for net command on fast surfaces, but will quite definitely pursue tactical mastery from the baseline on slow surfaces.

Apprentice Mixers

If you seek to become a mixer, you should first identify the one or two areas of your own game which are currently strongest. Perhaps you have:

★ A big first service and good forehand drive, *or*

★ a secure, sharply-spinning, first and second service, plus really electric mobility and a sound backhand, *or*

★ good volleys and overhead play, *or*

★ a splendid touch on drop-shot and lob and a good topspin forehand drive.

Recognize these strengths and then try to do two things.

1. You must use practice sessions to strengthen other aspects of your play and particularly try your all-round approach against weaker club colleagues.

2. You must, above all, keep your strengths strong – too many players who could have a prolonged competitive life at local club, or higher level, or a more effective tennis career, spend so much time strengthening their weaknesses that often their strengths weaken.

Pre-emptive Counter Attacking

One aspect of 'mixing it' will be on occasions to try to get to the net before the server does, or before a regular net rusher can get his approach drive played. Opportunities for this occur when a fairly determined net rusher has played a drive that he decides is not quite good enough to follow up to the net. The combination of his shot (assessed by its own executant as not being all that hot) and his possibly 'edged-in' positioning on court could give a splendid chance for a sudden net approach of your own, especially if you hit to the backhand.

Counter Attacking Established Net Command

A very confident mixer might regularly try this but even a moderate mixer should consider it. Do not always baseline against sustained net attack, banking on volleyer error, or passing shots. Instead vary your game by moving to the net yourself. As with any net approach, the shot preceding your move is the most crucial one and follows most of the rules of approach drives generally, the vital points here being:
(a) It must be low.
(b) It could well be slow.
(c) It will usually have topspin or slice.
(d) It will very regularly be straight rather than cross-court.
(e) It can be aimed straight at your opponent but then needs to be fast.
(f) It will only be angled if it is low – preferably very low and very sharply angled across the court.

Having played the preceding shot appropriately, you must move in fast and confidently following the ball to bisect your opponent's angle options (Diagram 19).

PLAYING AS A LEFT-HANDER

There are two probable reasons why left-handers have successes out of all proportion to their numbers. It is fairly obvious that left-handers are accustomed to right-handers' angles and strengths because they are constantly encountering them, whereas right-handers have to rethink on the occasions when they meet up with 'lefties'. Also, some neurologists and psychologists believe that the faster early development of the right side of the brain, the controlling hemisphere for left-handers, gives them quicker natural reaction times.

Confidence

Therefore, if you are a budding 'leftsider', go out there with confidence. Statistics and theory are on your side. You will have seen it all before when you play a right-hander, whilst he will often be feeling his way against this strange leftie, so do not waste those opening games.

Service

The huge advantage of left-handers is on service, especially when using a heavily sliced and angled service (Diagram 28). Not only does it drag a player wide out on the ad-court – the left court – but it is against the regularly weaker backhand and the hapless right-hander has to deal with a low ball and feels an unfamiliar spin on his racket strings. Even a player running into position has less room for his shot on the backhand (Diagram 29). Thus the receiver, from a more static pose, is doubly restricted.

Left-handers should use the slice service down the middle frequently in the deuce-court – the right court.

Left-hander's big gun

A major weapon in a left-hander's attack on right-handed backhands is the slice service.

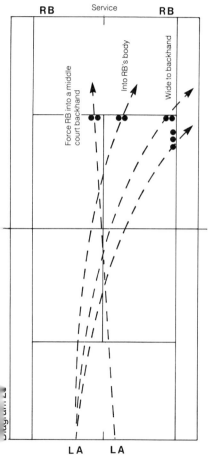

LA (left-handed server) can attack RB (right-hand receiver) in three main ways with well directed slice services.

Again such a service is bending like a banana at right-handed receivers' backhands, drawing them to the middle of the court and, on this side, narrowing angles of return.

Attack like this in the first game or two. Then, as the receiver adapts and counters with a wider position, start mixing in swinging slices to his body (Diagram 28). If you also have a good kick service and sensibly vary the amounts of spin used, you really can call the shots as a left-handed server.

Drives

Left-handers usually have good topspin forehands, across court over the lower part of net and homing in like a missile on to a right-hander's backhand. Your right-handed opponent is not all that accustomed to easing the ball down that backhand line to seek out your left-handed backhand – one of the riskiest shots in the game, as previously indicated. So, be merciless in unremitting forehand cross-court attack on your opponent's backhand.

Conversely, left-handers usually cause right-handers trouble with their backhand slice, because lefties get plenty of practice 'nudging' a backhand slice down to right-handers' backhands, by taking opponents' cross-court forehands early. Any down-the-line backhand off a cross-court shot carries an element of risk, but a left-hander can play it more confidently and with more margin for error, since he knows that he is edging the ball away from most opponents' big gun – the forehand.

Playing Other Left-Handers

This is where lefties themselves often need to rethink. Sliced service into the receiver's body is effective, especially into the deuce-court, often forcing a chipped backhand return with no real angles open. The widely swinging slice is less effective as left-handed receivers can stand square on to the net, yet still reach out and haul the services back with their forehands. Be aware when lobbing and alter your aim from the one you use against right-handers, otherwise you will present a left-hander with a perfect, smashable ball above his racket shoulder.

PLAYING AS A TWO-HANDER

Most double-handed strokes are on what would be the natural backhand wing. You probably commenced using the second hand on the racket to strengthen a weak backhand grip and the resultant 'scoopily' weak drive. So you are starting with a plus straightaway – the confidence that now you have a firmer and stronger racket-face on that backhand side.

Movement

Virtually everybody realizes that double-handers need to be very quick about the court, and the highly successful two-fisted players are all explosive movers. The one reason for speedy movement is clear – you cannot reach so far across the court as can a single-handed player – but there is another reason almost as important. Look at Diagram 29 and note how restricted is the swinging arc and especially the *contact arc* for a double-handed stroke.

Yet another reason is that two-handers find very high and very low balls more difficult, so you must move fast and precisely in relation to the ball's first flight and bounce. Never let an opponent's slow shot have the hypnotic effect of slowing down your footwork on any stroke, but especially on your two-handed side.

Power

If you position yourself accurately, a well timed two-fisted drive can have and should have fearsome power. You are not a real two-handed player unless you are 'asking the questions'. Just 'answering your opponent's questions' by using the second hand to keep a firmer racket-face on an otherwise disastrous backhand is not even half the story. You are still parading a weakness and running with restricted reach to an opponent's tune.

As a double-hander you should really add extra heat to the ball, as top players describe it, meaning hitting very hard. As a double-hander you should be constantly pressurizing opponents and if you are not really 'powdering the ball' check if your hands are close together and that your racket takeback is full and early. Followthrough is inevitably limited with two hands used but a good body turn will 'add the extra heat' that you need.

Disguise

The use of both wrists as extra leverage points in the swing gives tremendous racket-face and head

Comfortable and effective hitting arcs on the forehand, backhand and double-handed drives

If you stood high on one of the flood-lighting gantries and looked directly down on the heads of the three players you would see that:

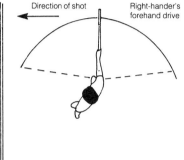

the *forehand drive* has almost a semi-circular range within which contact with the ball may be comfortably made in relation to the body, quarter-to-fully-sideways on to the net,

whereas

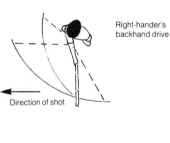

the *backhand drive* has a rather more restricted contact arc, due to the body getting in the way of the arm when playing the full swinging stroke, but has good front-on compensation range,

whilst

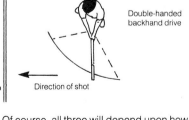

the *double handed backhand drive* has the most restricted hitting range of these three strokes; hitting points have to be very precisely chosen.

Of course, all three will depend upon how much the wrist is used to 'squeeze' racket head 'inside' ball or 'curl' it round outside of ball and will also depend upon how much racket head is dropped and how far body is turned. But in this matter of comfortable hitting points, the forehand has the more flexible 'side-on' range, the backhand is very flexible 'front-on', whilst double-handed strokes are the most restricted. Consequently, double-handed players must be good movers.

control and late flexibility, permitting disguise of direction until the last possible moment – so helpful in passing shots and in returning service.

Types of Two-handed Player

Study leading double-handers and decide which type you favour. Men usually are either committed 'crouchers and crunchers', or 'slingers'. The former hammer body turn and weight as well as racket swing into the ball, whilst the latter throw the racket into the shot, often releasing the top hand early after contact (inexperienced players should be aware of this if their accuracy is suspect).

Many ladies pivot in balletic fashion on the front foot; others press down on their front foot and force the racket into and through the ball. Your physique and personality will influence your approach to two-handed technique, but – experiment.

Controlled Movement in Singles

Whether you are a baseliner, a mixer or a net-cruncher, in singles you have to run fast, properly balanced, in the right direction and only as far as absolutely necessary. Controlled movement is tactical life for you and forced movement can be tactical death for an opponent. If you are heavily built and slow, plan to limit movement. If you enjoy running, do what is necessary but do not overdo it.

Playing a shot on the run is inevitable in many situations and is an almost continuous requirement of top-class play. However, it is obvious that a gun on a stable, balanced platform is more likely to fire accurately than one that is insecurely supported.

Logically, if you are on the run, in tennis terms it means that you are away from your headquarters in the centre of the net or your baseline, which, in itself, makes you more vulnerable. Additionally, the net is higher at the sides of the court, so begrudge movement forced upon you by an opponent and strive like a puppet-master to make your opponent dance to your tune.

Your Opponent

Categories of Opponent

Your opponent will fall into one of the following categories. He will be:

★ Well known to you and always beats you.
★ Well known to you and you always beat him.
★ A regular season-long battler with sometimes you winning, sometimes him.
★ Known to you even though you have never played each other (or at least not recently).
★ Unknown to you.
★ Unknown to you but of formidable and fearsome reputation, or reported to you as a 'pushover'.

Opponents come in all shapes, sizes, ages and conditions, some basing their game on McEnroe, others on Wilander or Navratilova or Evert-Lloyd, whilst still others are merely there for the 'fork-supper' afterwards!

Your opponent will therefore be:
* Strong and mobile.
* Strong and heavy.
* Light-framed but powerful of stroke.
* Light-framed and very agile.
* Very fit.
* Fit.
* Very unfit and looking as if he represents the Businessman's Luncheon Club.
* Very unfit and looking as if representing Oxfam.
* Older or younger than you.
* Really 'up' for the match.
* Not really interested.

Speculation
Overall advice on match preparation is given on pages 98–99 but, if the match you have next to play is anything more than a casual, or regular, very friendly 'friendly', your opponent will figure largely in your pre-match . thoughts. If it is a crowded 'short-set' type of competi-. tion, maybe a 'round-robin', you might only have a few minutes to consider your next adversary, but usually you will have at least an overnight chance of deliberation, often very much longer. So, what points should be occupying your mind?

Check how closely your thoughts agree with the advice given on the next few pages.

KNOWN OPPONENTS OF HIGHER STANDARD

Hit Him Hard and Early
If you have regularly lost to an opponent is there anything that you could 'hit' him with straightaway. Does he always slice his first service away to your weaker forehand or pound it down the middle on your backhand, 'serving notice' on you that he has it all planned out and is going to exploit your weakness to the full. What a surprise for him if you were ready for it and thumped it back, with some extra 'heat' added, as he confidently strides in to volley away your expected weakly chopped return.

Plug the Gaps
Is there a part of your game that he always manages to counter effectively? Does he use your pace? Then give him none. Does he outdo you on patience? Then take an early risk before getting bogged down in the nerve-racking rallies. **This time, can you still play the game you are best at but limit that area which borders on what he is best at?** Have you reasonable command of a different game and the ability to switch?

Did you fail last time because you crashed about one in three really good first services into court and volleyed well on those points, winning most of them but lost virtually all the other points which you commenced with a fault and then a weakish second service? Your opponent survived on your service, volleyed effectively after his first service but mostly outsteadied you from the baseline. Why not, this time, try slowing down your own first service and aim for 70% delivery into court, plus fast secure net-coverage; then on his second service make attacking returns, backed up by your net-approach? It is often only a very few points 'turned round' which transforms a 3–6, 2–6 type defeat into a 6–4, 6–3 victory.

Compound Interest
If it is just another match for him, but important for you and probably the only occasion that you will play him for some time, **let it all go in**. Try everything and if you should get the first set, play the second as if your very life depended on it. Early in this second set give him one or two golden opportunities for his favourite shot, or tactic, and be ready with your answers. If you win these points you have partially won the mental battle.

KNOWN OPPONENTS WEAKER THAN YOU

Be Prepared
Too many matches are lost because of casual confidence, which is a very close relation to arrogance. Your opponent might hit you early on with his 'dirty tricks department'. However many times you have beaten him, if the next encounter between you is a formally competitive one, then he has to be beaten all over again before you can polish the trophy, or think about knocking out the Number One Seed awaiting you in the next round. Even if the next encounter between you is social or

friendly, it is still important. You have to keep up your dominance on court as an ally for the next match when 'it really does matter'. 'How much it matters' is something you as the stronger player must be aware of as a danger point between you – perhaps this next game between you 'really does matter to him' – be warned.

Knocking up
Notice if the regular receiver of defeat at your hands seems especially alert and confident in the knock-up and appears to be doing something differently. These indicators could tell you that he, too, has been thinking about your regular victories and has a definite plan to thwart them. Alternatively, he might have had an intensive period of coaching and training and that weak backhand of his, which year after year in the club singles final enabled you to reap such a rich harvest of points, might have 'blossomed' in a way you will not like.

Your Game
Being aware and forewarned does not mean allowing him to dictate the game; quite the contrary. Play the game which has always beaten him and get into gear early, only modifying points of attack to other weaknesses if you find unexpected strength where previously there was only fragility.

UNKNOWN OPPONENTS

General Pre-match Phase
There will always be scores of glee-

ful tennis pavilion 'vultures' who will fearsomely pass on embellished opponent reputations. You will wonder why some reported stars are even bothering to play you, so impressive is their career record circulating in your club's bar. Ignore the drama but not the statistics. If it is your first season in the Winter League and the person you have to battle against tomorrow plays at a twelve-court city club, has thrice won the county championship and beat your stronger partner 6–0, 6–0, whereas you play for your village's second team, then you probably are in for a crushing defeat tomorrow. You could also be only 24 hours away from the most instructive and valuable hour to date in your tennis life. Most unknown opponents will not be 'aliens from outer space', so find out what you can about them.

Immediate Pre-match Phase (You as Host)
If he should happen to be coming to your club for the match, then you can use one of two methods. You could get there early, change, have a thorough practice on the very court you are to use, towel-down and disappear, leaving appropriate courtesy message arrangements with club staff, or colleagues. Then turn up punctually for the arranged time of your encounter.

Your alternative is to be a true host. Awaiting him, solicitous as to his well-being and his needs in the changing-room whilst noting his height, weight and stomach measurement, sniffing for any signs of embrocation which could give

away half-healed muscle pulls or just sheer anxiety as to this match, your ears alert for any wheezing sounds which could indicate his inability to last a long match.

Note the quality of his equipment and the style of his dress; even the way he actually carries his rackets will be a pointer to his tennis status. If he looks comfortable and natural doing some muscle stretching preparation he is probably not bluffing and really means business.

What the Knock-Up Isn't
The knock-up is *not* your warm-up practice hit for this match – you should have at least half-an-hour's warm-up practice in the hour or two prior to the match, where your personal/business timetable or the tournament schedule permit.

Using The Knock-Up
Obviously you are trying out all your strokes and getting the feel of the court, but observe him. Where does he put the ball? Is it nearly always short? Does he spin it severely, hit it hard – does he net a lot or hit out? Does he favour the forehand – does he let the ball bounce twice – how good a twister and turner is he? Return just a couple of his practice services (nowhere near him and more than a couple would be discourteous) but get the feel of his service-ball, its 'weight' and spin.

Note in which direction he smashes. In tough situations most opponents will play their favourite shot in their favourite direction, especially when smashing, so record this information and use it in the game.

Kid him a little – if you are agile, do not be over-active in the knock-up; if you have a weak backhand hit like mad on it and chip away on the forehand – you might be 6–2 and 4–1 up before he spots that it is your backhand which is your Achilles' heel.

Immediate Pre-match Phase (You as Guest)

Obviously much of the advice for this role is similar to that given to you as the host player but there are some differences.

Be certain that you know exactly where and when the match is to be played and for a strange venue allow at least 50% extra travelling time over the normal.

Quite apart from wishing to be free of any travel stiffness and being calm and relaxed, you will want to view the court surface and surroundings – get the feel of the place and above all get a long hit if possible *before* the knock-up.

Accept the fact that any opponent you see practising beforehand always looks way above your class. Forget these qualms; he is probably as anxious as you, especially if his club captain is watching.

Immediate Pre-match Phase (At a Tournament)

Far more likely, of course, is that many of your most important match encounters will be at an all day, a weekend, or a week of evenings, tournament and you will usually have opportunities to study potential opponents. If you are also enterprising and just slightly but courteously 'pushy', you should be able to *make* opportunities for good pre-match practice hits.

The First Point of the Match

If you are serving do not try for an ace off that first ball – the odds are so against it coming off. Neither you nor your opponent can be fully 'into the match' so what is wanted is to make that half-warmed-up opponent actually *to have to play the ball as soon as possible*.

If you are the receiver just concentrate on getting the ball well clear of the net and as far back in your opponent's court as possible, or near the server's feet if he is coming in. No hero-shots on that first point.

Playing Against a Left-hander

Recognize that it will be a different ball-game but need not be an unsettling one. Expect the spin to 'feel' differently on your racket; expect to be returning lots of services in the ad-court wide on your backhand and, in the deuce-court, near the middle of your baseline with no angles to work on – be ready to counter these strengths. Imagine the psychological advantage you will have if you do not play like a leftie's model victim.

Service Against Left-handers

If you have a good slice service, use it viciously in both courts and on first and second balls to slide away at the left-hander's backhand. Most players find the slice the easier of the two main service spins to impart. Against left-handers is the time really to use it.

Use 'Your' Diagonal

Get in first with a strong cross-court forehand to the left-hander's backhand, before the leftie can get the play going on the other diagonal. Slice a few drives at the left-hander's backhand and be ready for their slice to float up a little giving you an opportunity or two to kill the ball. Lob on the opposite diagonal to a right-handed smasher, ie on your right to his right diagonal (see Diagram 26).

Playing Against Two-handers

If he is a real 'powderer' of a ball but inaccurate, give him shots on the double-handed wing but get length on the 'pace-offering'. If you can also slip in a deceptive 'flight' and a touch of spin you should have a field day.

If he powders the ball accurately, then exploit his lack of reach and comfortable hitting arc by pushing him all over the court – up and down as well as side to side and force him to play shoulder-high drives or low ones in front of him. Really 'close down' the net when moving in against a double-hander – his late disguise of passing shot direction is more dangerous for you than his lobbing.

Soft Hitting on the Double-handed Side

This almost certainly indicates that the second hand is there to strengthen a suspect backhand. In these conditions it could pay dividends to attack that side ruthlessly, especially directing sliced approach shots to it and then commanding the net.

If you are playing a persistent slow-baller, lose your fear of lobs; get tightly in on the net and put the volley away for a winner.

Playing a Really Heavy Hitter (Right, Left or Two-Handed)

Ride with the pace early on like a boxer easing away from a blow. Do not try to pile on more pace. Avoid being mesmerized by the power build-up of your opponent's stroke but concentrate like mad on watching the ball off opponent's racket. Block many of these balls and once you get the feel of their weight on to your strings, start leaning in to your shots like a hill-walker against a buffeting wind.

Time and Rhythm

A big hitter needs recovery time and a steady rhythm – do not give him either. Do not allow him to force you way back behind your baseline; stay in there and press the ball back early at him. Do not trade long hammer-blow rallies with him but mix up the pace.

Playing Against the Floaty Stone-waller

Countering little pace sometimes causes inexperienced players more trouble than handling thunderbolts. Players tend to slow down their approach to a shot to fit in with the time available. Beware of two dangers in this when playing a floaty type of retriever. At one extreme some players will lose patience and make elementary mistakes, going to the net on ridiculous approach shots, or hitting the ball harder and harder and nearer and nearer the net and lines until an error creeps (or even crashes) in.

At the other extreme a player will move with so little urgency to answer a puff-ball drive that he finishes up playing the eventual shot as hurriedly as if it were a real rocket. You will have to generate pace on such shots but build up long and smoothly. Consider occasionally going in solidly to meet the lazily approaching ball nearly at the service line and *volley an approach shot* followed by net command. A few successes like that against such opponents and previous 'puff-balls' might get 'powdered' a bit.

Respect But Do Not Fear Opponents

The patient baseliner is a tennis competitor to be respected. You are opting out if you condescendingly say, 'Well, who wants to play a "hacker" anyway – if he can only win that way he's welcome to it. Good luck to him, but *I play tennis.*' It *is* good luck to him. He is playing tennis within the rules and *is too good a tennis player for you to handle.*

There is no divine authority indicating that tennis should be played in a manner pleasing and satisfying to a spectator's and opponent's eye. Providing gamesmanship is not used, a player employs any tactics within his control.

Control

Control is the vital word. If you categorize such a player as a hacker and justify a loss under that heading, he has controlled you, whereas in fact such a player has a limited game and you should control him. Like any good tactician he deserves to succeed if he can make you dance to his tune, so control your impatience and your awarding of soubriquets.

The Singles Match

Diagram 30 highlights the many major and mundane factors involved in a serious tennis match at any level. Tactics will be influenced by more than just how you and he like to hit that tennis ball.

SURFACE

Tennis is played on a variety of indoor and outdoor surfaces and there are so many trade names that it would be impossible to identify characteristics of each, but there are clear general types, varying according to use, cost and preference.

Grass

The original surface and superb for all aspects of play. The court takes slice on drives and service and 'kick' on service and favours a fast volleying game, but the 'live' grass carpet gives baseliners a chance of effective counter-attack. The limited season and cost of maintenance are its big snags.

Shale (Clay) Courts

The second oldest surface is the familiar red brick-dust court. It is semi-loose and water-bound, so again the snags are shorter playing availability and cost of maintenance. Players have to work for points on clay but it provides a medium-paced game. Speed will depend on how damp the surface is and the thickness of the top-dressing, so get a good feel of the court before the first point. This surface takes the sting out of first services and volleys and you need to keep the ball and your opponent running. The foothold is usually good and you can slide in emergencies.

All-Weather Courts

The best of these give a fastish game with true bounce, take spin and give a firm foothold but can be hard on the legs. Some can be slippy in damp or frosty conditions but modern compounds have overcome this. Synthetic grass, rubber or asphalt, are employed according to type and venue and many top sur-

faces are finished with a sand-filled paint.

More economical in cost is a graded aggregate bound together with cold bitumen emulsion and covered with a coloured grit, usually grey-green. This surface eases the jar on the legs and the grit skids the bounce, unless very thickly spread. The grit helps spin on what are generally fairly slow courts. You may often have to play on 'tarmac courts' (bitumen-macadam type) giving a very slow game but allowing reasonable tennis at a quarter of the cost of, say, synthetic rubber.

Indoor Surfaces

Most outdoor surfaces have at some stage been used indoors, either in sports halls, sports barns or air halls. Early indoor courts were mainly wood-floored and very fast but modern centres have permanent or movable rubber type 'carpets'. Some have rubber tiles and some replicate grass giving a medium fast all-court game.

THE SURFACE AND YOU

All players will have a favourite court but a real competitor will perform well on most surfaces. If the bounce is fast or uneven then you must volley as frequently as possible and utilize service to the full. On slower surfaces do not strive for unlikely aces when steadiness and accuracy are called for. Your tactics must reflect what you do best, what negates your opponent's best shots and what suits the surface best. Use the pace of fast courts to hurry the ball back to your opponent and take

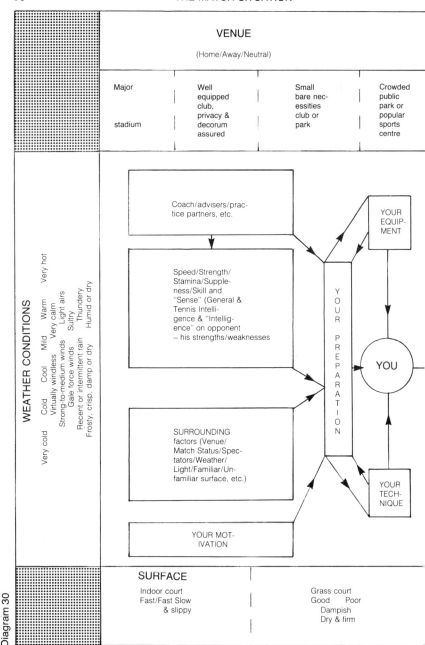

VENUE

(Home/Away/Neutral)

Major	Well	Small	Crowded
	equipped	bare nec-	public
	club,	essities	park or
	privacy &	club or	popular
stadium	decorum	park	sports
	assured		centre

WEATHER CONDITIONS

Very cold
Cold   Cool   Mild   Warm   Very hot
Virtually windless   Very calm   Light airs
Strong-to-medium winds   Sultry   Thundery
Gale force winds   Humid or dry
Recent or intermittent rain
Frosty, crisp, damp or dry

Coach/advisers/prac-
tice partners, etc.

YOUR
EQUIP-
MENT

Speed/Strength/
Stamina/Supple-
ness/Skill and
"Sense" (General &
Tennis Intellig-
ence & "Intellig-
ence" on opponent
– his strengths/weaknesses

Y
O
U
R

P
R
E
P
A
R
A
T
I
O
N

YOU

SURROUNDING
factors (Venue/
Match Status/Spec-
tators/Weather/
Light/Familiar/Un-
familiar surface, etc.)

YOUR
TECH-
NIQUE

YOUR MOT-
IVATION

SURFACE

Indoor court   Grass court
Fast/Fast Slow   Good   Poor
& slippy   Dampish
                                      Dry & firm

Diagram 30

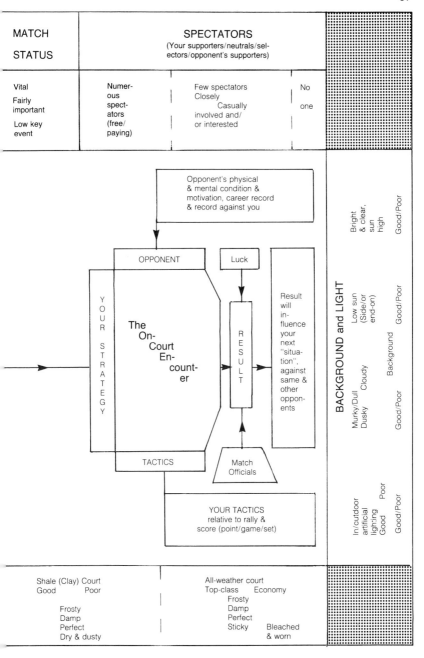

a risk to get to the net first. On grass, when you cannot command the net, pull out all the spins, dinks and lobs. On slow courts it will be the range, intensity and tempo of your tactics which are crucial to your success, especially tactics of movement.

WEATHER CONDITIONS AND SURROUNDINGS

Even indoor matches are affected by weather conditions. Varying temperatures will affect the ball and air pressure and surface bounce. Condensation can affect the foothold and the court's pace. Sunlight can be a hazard through windows. However it is more likely to be outside where the weather seriously influences your tactics.

Rain and Frost
Both will make an all-weather court slippy, so slice like mad, limit your own movement and move your opponent around as much as possible.

Heavy rain will make a shale court 'puddingy'. Turn this to your advantage with sliced drive, drop-shots and with shortish angled slowly hit drives which really pull an opponent out of position on low bouncing, slow courts.

On damp, soft grass use slice again to make the ball skid through unplayably low and be certain to bend low on all your own ground strokes in these conditions.

Temperature
There will be days when you feel that your touch has gone whereas it is merely that the balls are behaving slightly differently. New balls on a warm, clear day will travel faster and bounce sharply. They will seem sluggish on a cold day and swing more in heavy conditions.

Sun
It is not unsporting to lob frequently when your opponent faces a strong sun. You could effectively edge in when receiving service with the sun at your back and pressurize a double fault from a dazzled server. When you face the sun, focus on the ball not on the sky and let high lobs bounce. In very hot sunshine keep your liquid reservoir topped up, preferably with electrolyte drinks (see Appendix). Even a small fluid loss impairs efficiency.

Wind Behind You
Even prestige stadium courts appear to attract the quirkiest of zephyrs and you will frequently have to play in blustery conditions. Use a following wind by aiming first services for the net-band and make more adventurous moves towards the net. Be very careful when slicing approach drives that they do not 'hovercraft' their way out over the baseline, but use the wind's force to carry lobs high over an opponent.

Playing into the Wind
Hit lobs confidently into such headwinds and use the drop-shot to good effect. Apart from lobs keep the ball low in most wind conditions and restrict use of slice into headwinds which take all the pace from such drives.

Crosswinds

Right-handers should use angled slice services on right-to-left crosswinds. All players should leave enticing gaps on the leeward side. Often on the windward side you can 'bend a shot' around an opponent at the net by hitting courageously out over the sideline for the wind to blow the ball back in.

Rain and Poor Light

Always look as if you are enjoying it and even politely mention the fact. In poor light do your utmost to put in a good first service and aim for 100% when returning service. It is not unsporting to lob more frequently against a bespectacled opponent in a drizzle or to move a nervous runner about a slippy court. You play the shots most likely to win for you.

Surroundings

Do not allow an unusual background to upset you. The ball is most often sighted against the court surface, which can never be too unfamiliar, so concentrate hard on the ball's movement, your opponent and your plans for the match.

Spectators

These are not only part of the surroundings but also represent some external motivation, for you and/or your opponent. Maximum performance requires just the right degree of intrinsic and extrinsic motivation and the first few minutes of any match will almost inevitably see nervous errors due to over motivation, especially if there is someone in the crowd whom you (or your opponent) wish to impress. Concentrate on getting the feel of the court and the balls and the strength will return to your legs, as the adrenalin-induced pounding of your heart subsides. Beware of unexpectedly easy opening games against a respected opponent. Press in hard as there could be some factor in the surroundings lowering his standard and it could soon wear off.

THE MATCH ITSELF

The Warm-Up

Even before going on court do some mental rehearsal – get into a cocoon of concentration – and gently warm-up physically, flexing and stretching muscles over their playing range and getting to a level just below actual perspiration. A warm-up is just as important on a hot day and a warm-*down* after the match in all weathers is vital. Towel down thoroughly between matches and shower at the end of your playing schedule, gradually exercising over-used muscles down to zero. If possible avoid donning a tracksuit and sitting in damp clothes in a crowded, smoky atmosphere after a tough match, or a long drive home without changing.

Officials

Smile at the umpire when you first meet and particularly when he gives that first doubtful decision against you. Human nature being what it is, you are then highly likely to have the next doubtful one called in your favour. Players see what they expect to see but the umpire has been appointed the sole judge of fact and as soon as a ball is called out, *it is out* for eternity and cannot be altered by video-replays.

Get on with the Match

Put an umpire's calls in perspective. It is not as if the official is a doctor informing you that you have an incurable illness. That point has gone by but for a real tennis player the *next* ball coming towards you is always the most *important* one in your life. Forget temporary disappointment and concentrate on the next point.

Idols with Feet of Clay

If playing in front of a large crowd, neutral and/or partisan, beware of the 'faded glory effect' and also be ready to welcome it in reverse. Frequently everything – often outrageous shots and winners – will all go right for a player early on in a match to a crowd's delight. If Lady Luck is favouring you, do not push her too far – you could trap yourself into having to risk more and more to keep the crowd's adulation. Then when the opponent creeps ahead it could all turn sour.

If you are on the receiving end of a glamour boy hero playing winning stop-volleys off your best smashes take heart and heed – you are either on the wrong court, or it could all turn in your favour if you just stick at it in workmanlike fashion for a while.

Score

Next to your opponent, the score is the most important external factor influencing your tactical decisions.

Losing

If you are losing and nothing is going right just concentrate on getting the ball over the net one more time, then once more and so on. Blot out the overall score and concentrate on individual points. If this does not work imagine that you are giving your opponent some pressure training. Hit deep to the forehand, then deep to the backhand, convincing yourself that the rally is more important than who finally misses, nets or hits out. Be aggressive or defensive as normal but be a 'feeder' and forget your match anxiety.

Losing Heavily

Be alert to take advantage of a period when your opponent might relax. Be prepared to be more cautious if you are a wild attacking player well adrift on points. If you are a true defensive general, you will not need to be told that 2–6, 2–4 down is not necessarily 'curtains' for you. You might have ridden the storm and be steadily wearing down your opponent, but if you feel that stone-walling is not working, try to be more subtle in defensive play.

Trapped into an Opponent's Game

Attackers often fall into this snare, but defenders should also be alert to the danger. Very often a serve-volley player is crunching in the pace against a baseliner who is just lapping it up and winning on passing shots and on the volleyer's errors. Make your opponent run before going in and only go in on approach shots played by you from within your own court. Where the defender is trapped into an attacker's game, take a deep breath and refuse to be rushed into the passing shots. You do not *have* to hit passing shots with great pace. Go for the lines and do not flog at the ball but stroke it.

Neutral Display
Attacker or defender in such losing situations must try to present a constant 'display', like a TV test card, disguising feelings and shot intentions.

Vital Points
Some points *are* more important than others and champions win the big ones upon which matches turn.

Set Point (or Match Point) to You
If you hold a set point, do not blow it by excessive ambition, and beware of temptations to finish off with a real line-ripping ball. Do not think of spectators for one moment and do not think of winning too soon. Your opponent *has* to keep the ball in play or he has lost the set (or the match), so do not play into his hands and put the ball out for him.

In such situations, try not to 'choke' on your shots – hit out and aim long – avoid like the plague putting the ball in the net, or angled out over a sideline. If you have more than one set point in hand clinch it on the first – it gets harder as they slip by. Naturally a cushion of a couple of games or set points in hand will inevitably give you the confidence to be somewhat more aggressive, but still play that first set point as if it were your only chance.

Get your *first* service in and if

receiving, at all costs, make the server play at least one more shot – you *must* return that service – in a tense situation your opponent could well bestow on you the gift of an unforced error.

Set Point (or Match Point) against You
Keep assuring yourself that you are still there in the fight. Put your first service into play, or if receiving make certain you clear the net with that return. Do not try fancy angles. Against an opponent in the back court, as long as that ball is deep and in play you still have prospects. If your opponent is storming the net, providing your shot is not too high but clears the net you are still in business; leave any sharply angled efforts until you have a definite opening.

If your opponent has closed down the net and life is too difficult for a calmly stroked and aimed passing shot, lob high and deep, or if you should be close to your opponent, try one aimed hard at his right hip (left hip at left-handers). It saves you risking netting the ball or angling it out and it is the very devil of a spot from which an opponent might conjure a winner.

Having Caught Up
Quite often after a long haul back into a match, say from 2–6, 1–4 down to reach 5–all, a player relaxes. A good ploy to avoid this is to give your opponent his favourite shot to play (perhaps having plugged away at his weakness). Be ready for his answer and counter it. There are

three plusses in such a move: it will at least focus your thoughts away from relaxed relief; it could well surprise an opponent into error and, if he does play his crown jewel of a stroke and you steal the point off it, he will be a doubly dejected opponent. Again in such situations, security of first service and of return of service is paramount.

Having been Caught Up

Put all thoughts of missed opportunities out of your mind. Consider if you are being trapped into playing the opponent's game and if so, escape. You are still in there, your opponent could relax and the effort of drawing level could have taken much out of him. Be determined to hit courageously and fairly straight with lots of topspin (see pages 17, 99). It is difficult to put a ball out of court with topspin and the full driving of the ball should lift the spirits.

Set Score

If in higher men's play you are 2–1 down in sets, be thankful that you are still alive in the fourth set and let the fifth take care of itself. Your opponent might relax and give you opportunities for a shift in the balance of power denied you beforehand.

This happens sometimes in three setters (Mens' and Ladies') when a first set has been won. If you are a first set winner, or loser, fight like mad for those vital early games of the second set. There is no score in the world better than 2–0 to you in the second set whatever happened in the first.

Ball Change

In high level tournaments the balls will be at their softest in the vital seventh game of a first set and every ninth game after this. At lower levels balls are often changed after a set. Be aware of this in a close match, as stringing together some good returns of service on such games could give the crucial breakthrough. Be alert to this danger when you are the server.

The Tie-break

Be patient and tempt an early mistake from someone who has just pulled up on you. Even the very top players become cautious on that first tie-break point. However, you really must play those first two points determined to be 2–0 up. At Love-all, 5–all and 6–all, players feel that their legs just will not carry them so be extra particular about your footwork. Your concentration should already be in top gear and you require tunnel vision for that ball to the exclusion of all else. Play your strengths in a tie-break and resist out of character shots, such as a power player ambitiously attempting a precision drop-shot from the baseline. Use a well practised surprise but rely mainly on what you are at ease with in tight corners.

Final Set

You must start a third or fifth set looking and running as if you relish the prospect. The mind always indicates complete exhaustion before the body physically agrees with it – you would find the energy to run if the pavilion wall suddenly came crashing down on your court. If you had a good lead and have been caught up, the start of the deciding set is a dangerous period for you. It could see you disheartened for a vital point or two and it is too late to be sorry afterwards. An apparently disinterested approach could indicate to knowledgeable opponents and spectators that your subconscious had already opted out of the struggle even though you were not aware of it yet. If you have been taken to a decider at least you are still in there, so do not waste this second chance. If you have pulled back into a match from a hopeless situation do not relax – you still have to win.

Finally, in a fifth set, or indeed at any score in a match-situation, if you are mystified by the way things are going, try to pretend that you are controlling them.

The 12 Principles of Doubles Play

The primary objectives of doubles players in tennis will be exactly the same as for singles players. However there will be additional objectives for doubles:
1. To enjoy the challenge of combining well with a partner to form a successful team.
2. To explore different possibilities presented by Men's (Ladies') Doubles and by Mixed Doubles.
3. To extend one's tennis 'life' by playing a less strenuous form of doubles when any form of singles might be out of the question due to age. (Kitty Godfree – Ladies' Singles

The 12 Principles of Doubles

1. Put and keep the ball in play as severely as possible.
2. Command the net in order to make winning placements.
3. Get and keep together.
4. Keep in line across the court anywhere.
5. Try to limit the *time* you are separated.
6. Try to limit the *distance* you are separated.
7. Play on the weaker, or more 'exposed', or more unbalanced opponent.
8. When in command of the net, cover the danger areas and volley for a gap, or to open a gap. Otherwise volley at the opponents' feet and if in doubt aim down the middle.
9. If defending against opponents at the net, keep the ball very low, or very, very high.
10. Exploit the advantage of service.
11. Receivers should make the server play the third shot of most points.
12. Understand the value of surprise.

Champion at Wimbledon in 1926 – was still playing regular Ladies' Doubles in the 1980s!)

Much of the advice given in respect of singles firmly applies in doubles, too, but there are also considerable differences.

In doubles you are your partner's 'principal' asset and he is yours! Ideally, regular partnerships should examine these 12 principles together, as both must strive to adhere to them on court. In that way you are both far less likely to be each other's 'principal' liability.

1. Put and keep the ball in play as severely as possible.

Facts

(a) In *any* tennis plan, the aim is to get the ball over the net and into play as *severely as possible*.

(b) In doubles the plan has to go a little further – the aim of the ball-placement is to win the point if possible, or to bring your partner effectively into play, or to ensure that your partner is not exposed to attack. At first, though, the ball must go into play and if the only way you and your partner can get the ball into play again and again is to stand in No Man's Land (Diagram 16) and shovel it over, lob it, or push it, then do just that. Young or old however, this is merely a stage to be passed through as quickly as possible, if you wish to develop into real doubles players.

Conclusions

Limit own errors Put the ball into

play by service and return of service as severely as possible.

Force opponent error Keep putting ball into play as *severely* as the situation allows and aim to 'involve' your partner successfully.

2. Command the net in order to make winning placements.

Facts

(a) The *singles* court is 27 feet wide (8.23 m) and one player has to cover it alone, roughly 13 feet (about 4 m) on either side of the body.

(b) The *doubles* court is 36 feet wide (10.97 m) and two players have to cover it, with roughly *only* 8 feet (about 2.5 m) on either side of each player to be reached.

(c) High class doubles players (Men's/Ladies'/Mixed) are rarely seen hitting long baseline rallies at each other.

Conclusions

Taking the hill Many top players call going to the net 'taking the hill' and a single player's approach shots, volleys and overheads have to be of good standard to take the hill effectively.

You can take the hill in doubles Even on a slowish court and even at a comparatively low level of play, command of the net, if persistently sought over a reasonable period, must prove successful in doubles.

Photocopy the masters Aspiring players emulate top players' techniques and even attempt to copy their styles. Therefore, it is also essential to try to master their successful tactics. In Men's Doubles at virtually any recognizable standard and in Ladies' and Mixed Doubles at moderately high standards, the sole tactical aim, after getting the ball into play, is to direct it in such a way as to assist your partnership to command the net.

3. Get and keep together.

Facts

(a) There are four ways of moving on a tennis court:

  (i) *Lengthways*: baseline to net.

  (ii) *Lengthways*: net to baseline.

  (iii) *Sideways*: left to right.

  (iv) *Sideways*: right to left.

    (Diagonal movements are a combination of lengthways and sideways ones).

(b) **The rules split the pairs diagonally at the start of every point.** The server is required to make his delivery from behind a particular half of the baseline. As the receiver is only permitted to hit the ball after it has bounced in the correct service court, his position is also con-strained. The result is that those two players are diagonally opposite each other at the start of each point (Diagram 31). The rules allow the other two players to stand anywhere they wish – always providing that they are not on their opponents' side of the net!

(c) There are four 'team positions':

  (i) Both together at the net – overwhelmingly the best formation and position.

  (ii) Both together near the baseline.

  (iii) Both *in line* across court, anywhere.

  (iv) One up near the net, one back near the baseline. This is a recipe for disaster, or at least for difficulties except where it is a sudden unavoidable tempor-

Doubles positions (below)

Note the starting positions of all four players and the intensity of their concentration, even though this first service has been netted. 'Real' doubles should look like this at the start of every point.

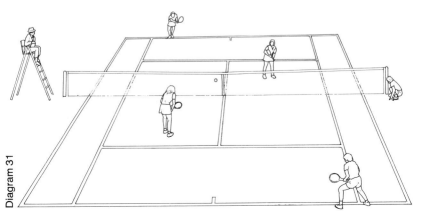

Diagram 31

ary positioning quickly rectified. Disaster strikes such positioning on an even greater scale if the opponents are together as a pair at the net.

Conclusions

Two's company at the net Tactics must be primarily aimed at getting command of the net as a pair.

If the worse comes to the worst If a pair is separated diagonally and the player further from the net just cannot progress forward because of opponents' severity of shot, the net partner must join up with the baseline player.

4. Keep in line across the court anywhere.

Facts

(a) There will be occasions when the very best of players will be moved out of position by their opponents' shots.

(b) Less experienced players frequently feel more comfortable and confident even in No Man's Land rather than right at the net.

(c) Very inexperienced players worry over who will look after the back of the court if both are at the net, or get anxious about drop-shots if both are on the baseline. Their solution is to cover the middle, one at the net, one at the baseline.

(d) Top players do not hang about in such areas or in such formations.

(e) The more often you are at the net the more at home you will feel.

Conclusions

Get in line (across) If you are unable to command the net together, at least keep in line across court with each other *anywhere*.

Caterpillars can become butterflies If you are very inexperienced and dislike net command, recognize that this fact is due to your inexperience and this must merely be a transitional stage in your tennis doubles life.

In the middle no-one is at home Covering the middle, one at the net and one on the baseline, ie more or less behind each other, cannot be all that advisable, as you never see a top pair remain in such an attitude for more than a fraction of a second. It allows opponents winners virtually anywhere in your court.

5. Try to limit the *time* you are separated.

Facts

(a) You are at risk all the time you are separated.

(b) Your shots can sometimes reach your opponent too quickly.

Conclusions

Minimize risk Play and direct shots that will help you link up with your partner, not split you further.

Delay risk If you are separated you must *buy time*, so do not neglect thoughts of a lob in such circumstances.

6. Try to limit the *distance* you are separated.

Facts

(a) If you stand in the same place twice you are bound to be wrong, whether or not it is you or your partner who actually played the ball. (b) The cut and thrust of the game will inevitably move you or your partner out of even good positions in order to play the ball.

Conclusions

Sympathetic moves towards your partner If, therefore, you do become separated by your partner's move to deal with a ball, not only must your partner be thinking of recovering to his original good position or adopting a better one, but you must also quickly match up sympathetically with him.

Be a successful managing director Height, speed and spin of your shot are important when you are separated but its *direction* is even more critical to your chances (Diagrams 32a/b).

Halve your differences If your partner moves any significant distance in any direction, you should move approximately half as far in the same direction. This broad guide will not do your prospects any harm and any movement by your team has to be noted and allowed for by opponents.

'Pig In the Middle' A good player moves to the *middle* of the net or of the baseline for only two reasons:

(i) either because an opponent's shot forces him there to play it, or

(ii) because he slips there quickly to crunch away a decisive winner.

Good players only *go* to and from the middle quickly, they never stay there.

Elasticated Rope A good doubles pair should always seem to have their waists connected to the same elastic rope.

7. Play on the weaker, or more exposed, or more unbalanced opponent.

Facts

(a) Unless there is a wide difference in the standards of your two opponents, the less dangerous opponent is usually the one farther from the net. There is an exception – a smash, or very easy high volley, is often best played by you hard and straight at the feet of the player nearer the net, who has less time to react.

(b) Where opponents are equidistant from the net, the less dangerous one is either the weaker player of the two, or the one still recovering from playing a previous shot.

(c) A shot going across the court takes longer than a straight shot, if the point of bounce in the opponents' court is roughly the same distance from the net.

There are really five 'grades' of shot:

(i) Desperate defence anywhere to get the ball back over the net.

(ii) Defensive retrieving, slightly limiting the opponents' options.

(iii) Shots exploring opening-up possibilities, or limiting opponents' options, when neither side has the upper hand.

(iv) Strongly pressurizing opponents with severe volleys, smashes, fierce or subtle driving, or lobbing, etc.

Percentage penning

With the two pairs in these positions, A could kill a high back-hand volley (from 1) to centre or to tramline (W), but the percentage low volley (from 1) would be over low centre net to area P to P.

If B has a high backhand volley to play, then a winner down the centre or to W are both definitely on, given the positions of the four players.

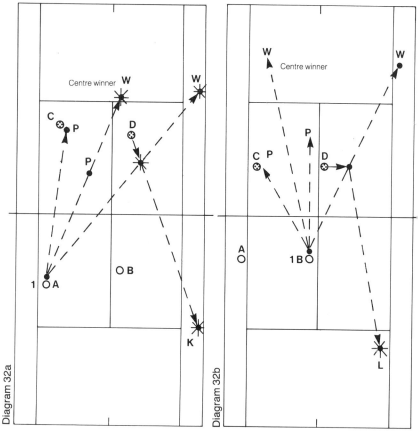

Diagram 32a

Diagram 32b

Off a low volley, if A tries to work ball to W, there is a danger of D killing anything weak to K, whereas replies from PP area are easily within B's reach.

However for any low volley by B (from 1), the percentage penning target is area PP, keeping ball nearer to partner A. Any indecisive aiming for W could result in losers at L from D's interceptions.

The elasticated-rope effect

If ball is to be played by opponent C in area 1, A and B should cover the arc 1 to 1, positioned about 8ft from net.

However, if ball is played by opponent D well to side of court in area 2, A and B should cover arc 2 to 2.

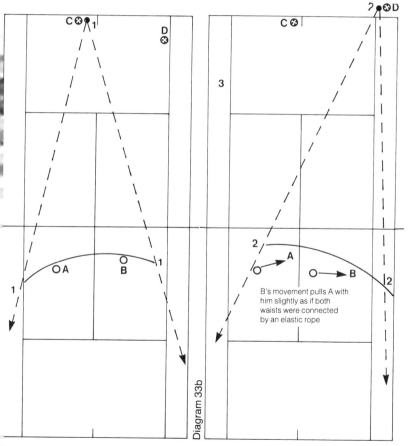

Diagram 33b

A and B positioned like this 'pack the centre' and restrict C and D to the riskiest angles over higher parts of net seeking tramlines, or force C and D to lob.

A and B are now covering the vital centre and the exposed right-hand tramline, both having moved right with A edging closer to the net. A similar move left would cover a ball being played from area 3.

(v) Taking clinically and efficiently opportunities for absolutely certain winning placements with smash, volley, drives, or lob.

(d) A diagonal system of play is inevitably set up by the service having to cross the court.

Conclusions

Remember what you did in singles You only *change* the angle for very good reason, ie you hit diagonally until an attacking opportunity, or a defensive necessity, dictate otherwise.

The Unbalanced Opponent The more 'exposed' opponent is likely to be the one farther from the net, or the one scrambling back into position after a previous shot.

No chivalry in the age of equality If it is a fifty-fifty situation regarding the best direction for your shot, aim lobs and smashes towards the weaker opponent and generally direct drives and volleys at the feet of the weaker opposing player (and that might well mean the weaker sex in a Mixed!).

8. When in command of the net, cover the danger areas and volley for a gap, or to open a gap. Otherwise volley at the opponents' feet and if in doubt aim down the middle.

Facts

(a) Downwards volleys from close to the net will usually win more points than upwards ones.

(b) The net is lower in the middle.

(c) There are three main gaps to be covered (Diagrams 33a/b).

Conclusions

'Close up' to 'close down' the net Close to the net means very close to volley down, whilst covering the two most likely gaps.

Packing the middle As a team, over-cover the middle at the expense of under-covering the tramlines.

Choose the soft centre If in doubt, volley down the middle.

9. If defending against opponents at the net, keep the ball very low, or very, very high.

Facts

(a) Good volleyers will deal with fast, shoulder-high balls easily.

(b) A fast low ball is better than a slow low one, but a slow low one is better than a slow high one.

(c) A very high lob, even if not deep into the opponents' court, gives time for your recovery and upsets the timing of less experienced smashers.

Conclusions

The lower the better Drive low and hard, or even slow and low, but no hard and high.

The higher the better Preferably lob deep, but lob high instinctively.

10. Exploit the advantage of service.

Facts

(a) You have two services.

(b) An opponent will have to be very good, or the service be very bad, for the return of service to be as effective off the first service as will be off the second.

(c) In doubles, the server's partner is standing near the net for easy killing volleys.

(d) Either partner may be the first of your side to serve at the start of each set.

Conclusions

First service pace versus percentages Attempt to serve a much higher proportion of first services into court even than you do in singles. Many star players serve in doubles at 70%/80% of their top pace in order to achieve 70%/80% first services into court.

Receiver's vulnerability Receivers are at their most vulnerable on the opening shot (service) and third shot (server, or server's partner's next shot) of any point.

Put all your eggs in one basket Always start with the stronger server and choose your side carefully to get that server the advantage of wind and sun etc.

11. Receivers should make the server play the third shot of most points.

Facts

(a) The server cannot get to the net until after the service has been delivered.

(b) The more dangerous opponent is the server's partner at the net.

Conclusions

Server's vulnerability The serving side is at its most vulnerable on the second shot (return of service) of any point.

Return of service The receiver should aim 80% of service returns dipping with topspin at the tramlines against the server running in, or severely deep and near the tramlines against the server standing back (Diagrams 34a/b, 35a/b). Vary the pace and flight of these regular diagonal returns, even, very occasionally, use chipped 'dinked' returns. Off weaker services sometimes aim at, or past, the server's partner at the net, or lob effectively.

Alertness as the receiver's partner Good angled returns at server (coming in, or staying back) often throw up opportunities for the receiver's partner to nip in and make a kill, on the rally's fourth shot.

12. Understand the value of surprise.

Facts

(a) Good doubles by its very nature does have a regularity which at times can become almost soporific.

(b) Most opponents will feel comfortable and at home with a regular uniformity of play.

Conclusions

Be disciplined but not predictable Keep to the efficient points-winning pattern of doubles play as indicated in the first eleven doubles principles, but do not become mundane and predictable.

If they have a lead give them a 'start' Success will go to the pair who can produce securely, especially at vital points, something their 'nodding' opponents do not expect to see – an unusual shot, move or formation.

Service and return of service in the deuce-court

A is server and C is receiver, B and D their partners, with brackets indicating alternative positions.

The receivers C and D should be firmly intending to follow C's return into the net.

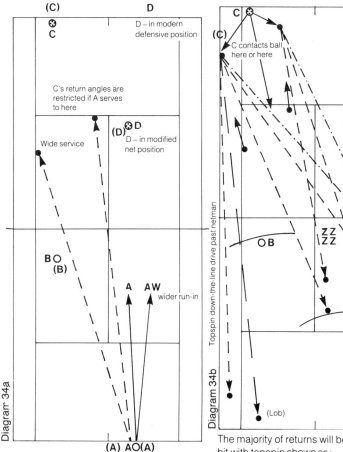

Diagram 34a

Diagram 34b

In doubles in deuce-court most services will be down centre but should occasionally be swung wide, in which case A should 'shade' wide to AW.

The majority of returns will be cross-court, hit with topspin shown as : – – – – →
Lobs: ——— ——— ———
Dinks: —·—·—·— —·—·—·— →
Player's movements: ———————→
Bounce of service ball: ●———→

Service and return of service in the ad-court

A is again server but this time to D receiving in ad-court.

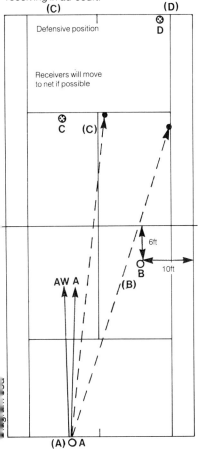

Service will be more evenly spread in ad-court, as A will aim 50% for D's backhand. In both courts, centre-theory serving allows netman B to press more for the middle and shield server during server's run-in.

Again, the majority of returns, topspin or dinked, will be cross-court but, if netman (B) moves too soon, the down-the-liner or the lob are always possibilities.

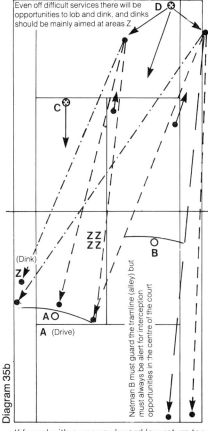

Diagram 35b

If faced with a very awkward low return too difficult to volley or even half-volley, server should halt run-in at A (drive) and drive short and sharply back across court to more vulnerable opponent, receiver D.

Get acquainted with the unusual Time spent practising such ploys as 'the American formation' and trying out the switch of the net player and server, on the server's run-in, could well tuck a match-point under your belt and see you on the way to the engraver's with that precious cup (Diagrams 38 and 39).

Summing up These Principles
Comparison of singles and doubles indicates broadly that singles is a game of *length and individuality*, whilst doubles is a pattern of *team-work and angles*. Men's Doubles of any quality at all will have the four players in rat-a-tat volley confrontation near the net for much of the time. The very best Ladies' Doubles will be similar but less competent ladies will seek net command more cautiously; however, they should very definitely seek to dominate that net. Mixed Doubles is a real battleground – the perfect vehicle for a mixture of tactical individuality and imagination, but still within the definite net-seeking pattern of all doubles play.

Pairings and Teamwork

Marriages might be made in heaven but doubles partnerships start rather lower!

Pairings
You usually team up with a long term partner because you like his standard or style of play and you feel comfortable together. You will also frequently be paired with another player by the captain or other persons in charge of various teams. In either case you might enjoy your tennis in such partnerships even if not successful and that in itself is a good enough reason, but naturally you will usually derive greater satisfaction from the team effort of doubles if you regularly win.

Temporary Pairings
These are features of tennis doubles at semi-social club events and at tournaments if you enter as 'wanting a partner'. It is normally a case of doing your best with whoever you have, although some remarkable international successes in doubles have arisen from casual initial pairings.

Mixed Doubles
The selection process is sometimes based on non-tennis criteria and success is not always judged in tennis terms!

Weaker Players with Strong Ones
Fellow competitors frequently indicate that a certain player only won because of his strong partner. That is a great compliment to the weaker player as, presumably, unless there were unusual reasons for the pairing, the weak one snapped up the good prospect early or the good one could find no one stronger.

In either case, if the partnership won, they were good enough as a team to beat everyone else.

Teaming up

There are some specific points that may be usefully considered in teaming up with another player.

1. A 'schemer', who sets up good openings, combines well with a 'finisher'. The schemer steadies things in a crisis and the finisher dominates play when his pair is on top.

2. Three-quarters of a player's time is spent in one half of the doubles court. Players should, therefore, decide early and with care whether they are going to be right or left court receivers of service. Note the guidelines on page 87.

3. Some partnerships are close friends, others virtual strangers off court. What is important is the on court recognition of the objectives of doubles play and an understanding of a regular partner's strengths and weaknesses.

Two simple examples highlight different, unsympathetic approaches to a partner's basic playing pattern.

A heavily built, slow mover crashes in a big service and follows up with a strong volley; the opponent's desperate return hovers near the big server's cautious partner who plays safely and does not volley severely; the opponents recover and angle the ball out of reach of the big slow mover who looks to be to blame for the lost point, but isn't!

Just as unfortunate would be this scenario. A slight, safety first player risks all on some good first serving only for his stronger partner to pound two glorious looking volleys just out to go Love–30 down. The power player thinks that an easy score to pull back with a couple of big services but to the cautious partner Love–30 is a mountain to climb!

4. Partners should talk to each other before matches and between points. On court limit this to encouragement and brief indications of desirable tactical change. Occasionally have a quiet but obvious word about nothing to convince your opponents that you have a cunning surprise all planned.

5. Doubles is a very structured game. Both partners must acknowledge this and limit any individuality of approach. The aim is to involve your partner immediately from the service or the return of service and genuine teamwork is the essence of successful doubles.

Teamwork in Doubles

Obviously your response to the following advice will depend upon your standard of play, your motivation (internal and external), your age and your personality but, however many doubles matches you have played, still read this carefully. Frederick The Great had two mules that had accompanied him on every campaign but, he would observe to his unthinking officers, they were still mules.

Have a Plan

You must have a simple plan – nothing complicated and discussed hurriedly minutes before you go on court.

Consider the 12 principles and sink your individual likes and dislikes in a joint endeavour to keep to these principles.

Within this plan, be comfortable and natural aiming to bring your strengths to bear on the opponents' weaknesses.

Command the net as a pair and be with each other in body and spirit, not one slaving away on the baseline, whilst the other lolls at the net mentally downing a drink in the pavilion.

Preparation

Both players must want to play that particular match, although there will be occasions when you will just have to carry a reluctant, even truculent, partner.

Make certain that you know exactly where and when you are playing, as an apprehensive partner changing alone might not transform into a dependable rock at match point.

Decisions

Certain vital decisions must be made beforehand:

(i) Who is to serve first in each set. Do not just take it in turns.

Read the rules and note that each set is a separate compartment for the service order. The stronger server should always serve first in every set, unless the sun would thus be in a left-hander's eyes, or other reasons prevailed. The fairly common score of 6–3, 4–6, 6–4, should see the stronger server of the winning pair deliver 50% more services than the weaker partner.

(ii) Who is to serve at which end? You usually bank on holding the

stronger player's service so he has all the advantages of shade and wind. Weather conditions vary and your opponents' choice after winning the toss might be unexpected, so give a moment's thought to your best options before striding purposefully on to commence the warm-up.

A right-hander's slice service is helped by a right to left wind but his kick service would be assisted by a left to right wind.

Take special care over your options if one of you is left-handed.

The Knock-up (Hit-up)

This is similar to singles but there are extra considerations for doubles:

(i) You will immediately show your inexperience if you attempt to hit up as a four. Always warm up as in Diagram 36. Usually your right court player hits with the left court opponent and vice versa.

In Mixed the ladies hit together as do the gentlemen.

(ii) Be certain to play some volleys and smashes and practise service from right and left courts.

(iii) Try to observe which opponent looks the stronger and/or really keyed up for the match and then in a crisis be sure to hit to the weaker or less interested one.

(iv) In a Mixed the lady is usually considered to be the weaker and there should be no sentiment about serving severely to her or attacking her service. Real Mixed competitors will expect this and will be trying to do the same to you.

(v) Get your concentration going from the first ball of the hit-up.

Looking the part in the knock-up and sun's position relative to court
Do not show your inexperience by attempting a doubles knock-up as a FOUR!

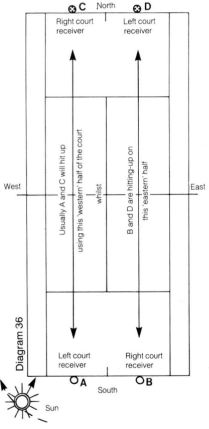

Diagram 36

Position of sun could affect service order, especially if a left-hander is playing. See advice on this on page 100.

Choice of Receiving Court

This is an important tactical decision to be made quickly by temporary pairs but is usually well established in regular partnerships. You spend 75% of your time in your chosen half of the court, so specialize urgently.

At an early level everyone will opt for the right court, fearing for their weak backhands in the left court but one has to play on the left and these pointers should guide your decision:
(i) The man almost always plays on the left in Mixed Doubles.
(ii) At inexperienced levels the stronger player usually plays on the left.
(iii) Left-handers normally play on the left.
(iv) A strong double-handed backhand is effective in the left court.
(v) A player with a blistering cross-court forehand is more effective on the right.
(vi) Similarly good backhand players favour the left.
(vii) Remember that:
★ About 10% more points commence with a service to the right court.
★ The overwhelming number of game (set/match) points are served to the left court.
★ Smashes are easier for right-handers to play when in the left court.

Conclusion

Be single minded about playing as a team in doubles.

Practising and Playing Doubles Roles

Role Playing

In doubles the role you have to play is pretty sharply defined for you, whereas in singles, as we have seen, you play the role which most appeals to you and is appropriate to your personality, physique and age.

Obviously, in doubles too, age will slightly diminish avid net-rushing but that is the overall role which you must play – a hungry volleyer you must be in anything but the lowest levels of any type of doubles play.

Within this net-commanding role, four specific initial roles are placed upon you by the rules governing service order and receiving order.

They are:

Your role as server
Your role as server's partner
Your role as receiver
Your role as receiver's partner

Practising these Roles

As with singles, discovering these roles and their 'duties' on court is only the start of your improvement. You have to go out there and quite specifically practise the moves and shots called for by these roles.

These four major aspects of your play as an aspiring doubles star are, therefore, considered in a practical on-court way. With just *one* willing opponent such practice can be painless and enjoyable and consequently productive; with three others it can be doubly so.

Your Role as Server

(i) Practise *directing* your service as in Diagrams 34a/b, 35a/b and aim to get 80% of your first services in. Give attention to 'centre theory' and get more height over the net by increased spin, especially on second service.

(ii) Practise approaching the net *immediately* to be ready and balanced for your first volley, an absolute must for males, or getting in as soon as you possibly can if female – certainly no more than one drive. Note the slightly wider run-in. Because you have a partner covering the one side, you 'shade' away from a wider-angled service when running in, not towards it as in singles.

(iii) Practise placing difficult low volleys almost 100% diagonally and kill all high volleys, again mostly diagonally.

Serving Team's Command of Net in Doubles

The vital move for server in doubles is to reach the net as soon as possible after serving.

Note how server has picked up a half-volley en route to the net; mind and body obviously intent on keeping moving forwards to the net.

The shot (short-drive, half-volley, low-volley, or higher-kill) must be played effectively without impeding that inexorable netwards thrust.

See how server has joined with netman, both in line across the court.

Observe how both players have eased their weight backwards, moving in unison like puppets on the same string, as one prepares for a possible overhead smash. This is *real partnership* in doubles.

(iv) Practise turning potential half-volleys into low volleys.
(v) Practise getting your partner 'involved'.

Your Role as Server's Partner

(i) Practise standing nearer the centre than the side of the court, except possibly in the left court if your partner has a regular, severe kick-service to your opponent's backhand.
(ii) Practise hitting volleys from close to the net, not letting the ball come travelling on into your court, especially if the server has put pressure on the opponent in the right court by serving down the centre to the receiver's backhand.
(iii) Practise decisive action at the net, ie let few lobs bounce; do not nibble at a shot and then let it go through to a startled partner, and make your *first* volley your *last* of any point, nothing fancy and enjoyable, just a clean, ruthless winner.

Your Role as Receiver

(i) Practise taking an early, rising ball and hitting regularly with top-spin hard at the server's feet and/or aimed at the junction of the service line and tramline (Diagrams 34a/b, 35a/b). This is of more value than standing back hitting rallies of 20 or 30 shots with a practice partner.
(ii) Practise 'reading' the service and predicting its dangers and weaknesses, blocking the really tough ones and error-free attacking of the slower ones, especially second service.
(iii) Practise moving in immediately to the net after returning service –

remember, never play two drives in succession in doubles. Practise making your return a winner past your opponents, or a hot-shot that gives your partner an easy kill off the next ball, or a shot that lets *you* get to the net.

Your Role as Receiver's Partner

(i) Practise watching the server's partner, covering any possible interception by him or her; then as soon as it is obvious that your partner's return of service has gone across court to the server, move in fast for an interception opportunity (Diagrams 41a/b).
(ii) Practise moving to cover a wide stretched receiver, 'the elasticated rope' (Diagrams 33a/b).

All Players

(i) Practise moving – stand in the same place twice and you are inevitably in a wrong position. This applies especially to the non-hitting partner.
(ii) Practise finishing every rally right at the net, win or lose.
(iii) Practise keeping out of, and getting out of, No Man's Land. Give particular attention to practising those crucial doubles shots – service/return of service/low volley/smash/lob.
(iv) Practise accruing points like misers; begrudge every point lost, especially at Love-all.
(v) Practise, and think of, *interceptions* as only *winners*.
(vi) Practise changing side in defensive situations, but limit this in matchplay to the minimum (Diagram 37).

SPECIFIC PLAYS

There are certain plays that prove successful in doubles over and over again. As indicated the two most obvious are:

1. *Serving side* Good first service, usually to centre in 'deuce-court' and regularly to centre in 'ad-court'; server follows in to net or at least tries to get there after no more than one drive.

2. *Receiving side* Mainly cross-court return of service, low and dipping and an attempt to snatch net command from the serving team or at least to join servers at the net in a volleying exchange.

There are, of course, additional playing patterns, particularly those occurring as the rally develops beyond service, return and first volley.

Receiver's Partner In Defensive Position

In the last quarter of the nineteenth century, as tennis developed, doubles pairs started on the baseline. Then as Men's Doubles developed, the server's partner came in to stand at the net and around 1903 the Doherty brothers *received* service with the *receiver's partner* in what is known as the *modified net position* (Diagrams 34a/b, 35a/b).

Recently, against fierce first serving on some of the modern synthetic surfaces, giving receivers a chance of a drive or two, the receiver's partner has again adopted the defensive position (Diagrams 34a/b, 35a/b) moving in as soon as the opportunity occurred. This very

sound tactical formation should, however, only be used against first service and even then not all the time. **The aim must still be eventual net command.**

Packing the Centre

This 'packing' of the middle gap on a doubles court at the expense of the two sideline gaps definitely does *not* mean one player in the middle and the other behind him. It means edging a little closer to each other across the court to cover the middle and force opponents to go for a risky angle.

> *As a guide*
> *Stay back and wide,*
> *But squeeze up tight*
> *With the net in sight.*

Penning the Ball

In a way the ball, and your opponents have to be kept 'penned' like sheep. In doubles (as in singles) a cross-court shot played from the baseline with its longer distance to travel and with a lower net at the centre can be your friend if both you and your partner stay on baseline, or better still both move to net together.

But when playing a shot close to the net there are two dangers with angled attempts. You can overdo the shot and spill the ball out over the tramline. You can also open up an angle that gives an opponent a chance for a quickly-taken volley into a gap before your pair can reassemble your line of defence (Diagrams 32a/b).

Therefore, it is wise to think of

'penning' opponents when in any doubt and to think of angles in two ways. Because of the wider court, doubles is a game of angles and fairly severe angles should be used to open up the opponents' defence line – with very severe angles being played mainly when easy opportunities occur for outright winners.

Covering For a Partner

At the top level, players usually smash or chase lobs over their own half of the court. Occasionally, however (more frequently at lower levels) the partner (Player B in Diagram 37) is better placed to move and pick up a good lob. The other player (A) must immediately hurry to cover the partner's empty side. B cannot be anywhere else until he has played the ball at position X, so it is up to A to move at once to provide cover for the other main danger areas, Y and Z. Note how C and D followed C's lob into the net and packed the middle, D being five to six feet from the net and C no more than eight feet from the net.

Surprise Formation

The One-Sided or Reversed Service Formation is a useful counter to a sizzling cross-court return of service in the deuce-court, which might be causing the incoming server trouble (Diagram 38). The server must move into the net very quickly. The receiver's partner should edge in towards the net slightly and also towards the middle. The receiver should aim for a really severe ball down to A's backhand. An alternative for a receiver is a diagonal lob.

Covering when partner lobbed-movement of all four players

C and D move to net after C lobs A.

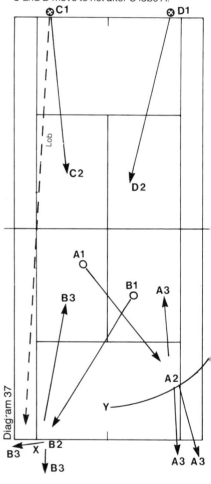

Diagram 37

B meets C's lob at X whilst A has moved to cover YZ arc. A and B's next position (3) will depend upon quality and type of B's shot, probably a lob. If good A and B return to net; if poor they stay back.

The one-sided or reversed service formation

Note server's close to centre position (A1) and likely service target area (XX). Note amended positions of B and D.

Server's partner's poach (or 'drift')

B has a better 'poaching' chance if A serves to XX rather than YY.

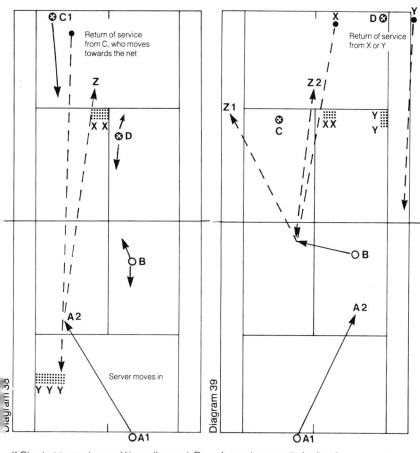

If C's shot towards area Y is really good, D will crowd in and B will edge back. If C's shot is poor, allowing A to volley severely perhaps to Z, it is B's chance to crowd in and D must retreat.

A runs in normally for first few paces then veers right to reach A2.. If B times move well he should, at least, have 'killing' opportunities to Z1 or Z2.

When used in the ad-court, the server has an easier role as he is moving in on a comfortable running-line for a good forehand volley. The receiver should therefore not strive for too much angle – aim fairly straight but low and again consider a deep diagonal lob.

Scissors Movement or Drift

As in Diagram 39, the server should run in normally for two or three paces before veering right. The server's partner at the net must not 'drift' too soon, but must go decisively, with no change of mind which would obviously leave the server stranded.

Providing the receiver hits firmly enough or early enough the 'drifter' (Player B in diagram) is unlikely to be able to volley the ball very far in front of his body-line, so almost certainly will then go for the area Z1 to Z2. The receiving pair's main task, therefore, is always to give priority to covering that danger area.

Server's partner B should always be aiming to reduce pressure on server A by subtle body movements feints, etc., and generally make a thorough nuisance of himself at the net.

GENERAL POINTS

Statistics

The average number of points in a game is six and except on very slow courts the rallies average out at about five shots per point. Of these 30 shots in each doubles game, the server will play over 12 on average and the receivers about seven or

eight each, so the server's partner must keep alert for his meagre share – and more. Apart from service and return, the most commonly used shot is the volley, many of these being low volleys, so practise this shot (Diagram 40).

Service and Return of Service

One break of service will win many good doubles sets, especially in Men's Doubles, and as a huge proportion of the serving side's points accrue after a first service has commenced the rally, you should make a real effort to get that first ball in. The likelihood of getting an error on return of service off a first ball is about five times that from a second service ball. On fastish courts about 30–35% of doubles shots are services, or around 50% if one counts faults as shots.

First Volleys (Server's and Receiver's)

Taking a good opportunity to angle away a high return sees the server eventually winning 70% to 80% of those points. A deep first volley off any return is a three times better bet for winning the point than a short one.

If the server volleys upwards to give the receivers a high first volley, the serving side's chances of winning the point are suddenly reduced to below 30%.

Similarly, if receivers can get in to the net after return of service and volley deep or at the serving team's feet, they are overwhelmingly favourites to win those points. On the other hand, they will lose over 60%

Low volley practice
A and practice partner B start outside service courts then play in service courts only, diagonally or straight. A feeds off a low ball underarm and both players move in.

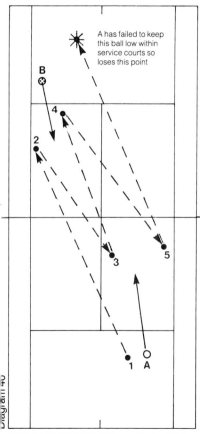

A has failed to keep this ball low within service courts so loses this point

B

4

2

3

5

1 A

Both A and B hit sharp low volleys whilst pressing forward to the net. Score as tennis, using left diagonal for odd points, or use table tennis scoring. Four players could play in all four courts.

of points when their first volley is short and over 70% if their first volley rises high at their opponents.

Return of Service Intentions
The receiver should try to hit all three options without giving a clue as to his intentions: cross-court fast firm and top-spinning; cross-court 'dinked' at the server's feet; or lobbed over the server's partner. A surprise fourth option is fast and straight at the server's partner at the net, or straight down the tramline past the netman. Deception is the ability to avoid giving any advance clues (cues) to one's opponents; a receiver who can play these three main returns of service with almost identical preparation is going to cause the serving side trouble.

Taking Your Time as Receiver's Partner
As soon as the service lands (sometimes even before it does so) you, as the receiver's partner, must be planning your move and as the receiver hits the ball you must be in action too. Look at Diagram 41a in which receiver is B and you are A, his partner. Imagine that you are standing on a large clock-face and that your partner B is standing on an even larger one; both clocks are tilted slightly towards each other.

Any movement by you out from broadly 3 o'clock to 7 o'clock will be largely influenced by how much your partner has been drawn out from his 'clock' and at what 'hour', mainly 2 to 4 o'clock and around 9 o'clock. On the other hand your forward movements and the dis-

'Taking your time as receiver's partner'!

In the deuce (right)-court
You are A and your partner B is receiving service in the right court.

In the ad (left)-court
You are A and you are receiving service in the left court.

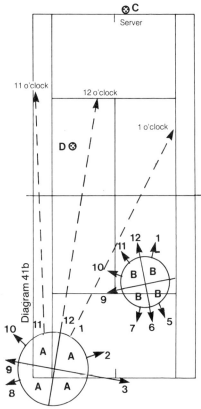

If B aims for 11 o'clock you track out 'on' 11 o'clock too. If B is drawn out of position try to be only 'an hour or two' away from him!

Expect your partner B to synchronize many of his movements to your moves and/or relative to the general direction of your shot. For advice on movement as receiver's partner see page 90.

tance moved will largely depend upon the severity of your partner's shot and the 'hourly' direction from his clock. If B hits on a line out from 11 o'clock, you move on a line from 11 o'clock on your clock; B hits to 12 o'clock, you move on a 12 o'clock line, etc.

Certain times, of course, just do not synchronize, or would involve bizarre movements, but the basic concept should get you 'ticking'! In the left court with you, as receiver A, having the larger clock and your partner B the smaller one (tilted towards each other), the same principles apply (Diagram 41b) so make certain that your partner's clock is *fast.*

Conclusion

Personal weaknesses of technique may be much more easily covered up in doubles than in singles but personal idiosyncrasies that work well in singles are not so permissible in doubles. Successful doubles involves teamwork within the main pattern of doubles play and the discovery by your team of the 'power centre' of the opposition; a particular 'play' of theirs; a stronger player; a hustling pace; a breaking up of your line to expose a diagonal or a soft middle. Whatever that power centre is, it must be ruthlessly eliminated.

You must avoid the 'exposed diagonal'
In doubles you must avoid the 'exposed diagonal'. Here A and B are in danger in every direction.

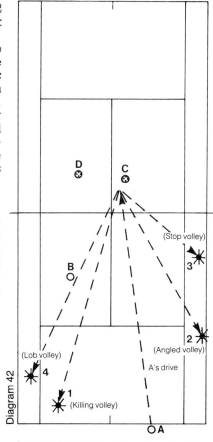

Shots by C to 1, 2 and 3 are almost certain losers for A and B if A's drive is high. Even the lob volley (4) over B could spell real trouble for A and B, split as they are on court.

Strategy

Your grand strategy must determine where you place tennis in your life but even a modest involvement in the game will be more enjoyable and worthwhile if you have definite objectives. Decide broadly what you require from the next few seasons and plan your strategy accordingly.

Information
Analyse your current game to know more certainly your starting point. Get someone reliable to record the statistics and features of your playing pattern along these lines:
★ Were your service faults mainly netted, or out over the sideline or service line?
★ What were your first and second service statistics to right and left courts?
★ What were the statistics on your return of service (cross-court/ straight/lobbed) and on your volleys and smashes in terms of placement winners against errors.

Intelligence
Analyse the games of your regular opponents and try to discover the main moves and counter-moves which occurred on crisis points – those vital one or two points on which the result so often hinges.

Reconnaissance
Often the first sight of an opponent is in the warm-up, so put at least two or three balls dead centre at him. His movement to make forehand or backhand returns will frequently indicate which he considers is his stronger side.

Training
Speed, strength, stamina and suppleness are your basic ingredients as a tennis player.

Do not train for training's sake but remember that fitness levels have to be maintained.

What You Can Do
In preparation for a season, build up with basic exercises of the early morning type done by the healthy brigade.

Add in an on-court exercise (Diagram 43) and every few days do a 12-minute run. Commence this run gently and *gradually* extend the distance that you can cover, jogging back after 12 minutes.

This plus the Running Drives practices and practice matches will set you up for the main campaign.

Off-days
Everyone will have off-days and *the good player is the one who wins when not playing at his best.* Never use an off-day as an excuse, even to yourself. Your opponent may have had one of his off-days and still has beaten you.

Diet
Serious tennis players should strive for a diet strongly featuring fresh fruit and vegetables and their juices, salads, fresh milk, oat-flakes, soya-beans, cheeses such as Brie, wheatgerm and yoghurts. Not everyone likes the same food and regular eating habits are often disrupted by match schedules. Some 'fast' foods make you 'slower' (see Appendix).

On-court potato race

Pick up balls separately from 'stations' 1–6.

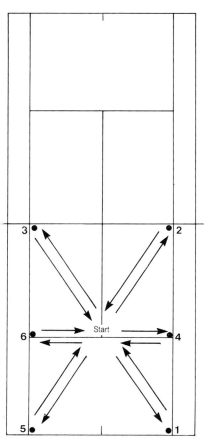

Place balls down firmly at centre, or at 'stations' when doing 'race' in reverse. Sometimes do the exercise running backwards with ball, or forwards empty-handed.

Equipment

Take care over your appearance and over your choice of rackets and footwear.

Rackets are getting larger in the head, with increased sweet spot for hitting, thinner gripped and lighter. When shaking hands with your racket there should be a gap of about ½" (12.7 mm) between the tip of your fourth finger and the base of your thumb.

Fast, whippy players favour thinner grips. The wrong grip size can cause tennis elbow.

On Court Strategy

Although you might use temporary tactics to upset a particular opponent, your overall strategy must be balanced and suited to your type of game.

Early Rounds

Win them all 6–0, 6–0 if possible, as certain reserves within the body cannot be made up quickly in some repetitive competitive situations and you do not want to hit the wall (ie run out of glycogen in the muscles) in the final.

Later Rounds

As a finalist be politely pushy to ensure reasonable on court practice before your big match, but in the final be anything but pushy. Follow Martina Navratilova's advice and avoid choking on your strokes by hitting out fully with masses of top-spin laid on.

Doubles Strategy

Poor tactical decisions in singles can

be covered by guts and bluff but in doubles only true team strategy is rewarded. For example, stop-volleys would fit a doubles plan but drop-shots usually would not. Specialize as a right or left court receiver and ensure that your stronger server always serves first.

When a right-hander and a left-hander are partners avoid either having to face the sun when serving.

Doubles Signals

Agree on these beforehand as you do not want your clever, tantalising lob startling your partner more than the nervous opponents.

Captaincy

The main tasks are:
1. Team selection and ranking.
2. Matching styles, strengths and receiving specializations, to ensure compatible pairings.
3. Assessing the opposition and planning the team's match approach.
4. Organizing practices, encouraging struggling sides and restraining victorious exultancy.

A Sound Strategy

This is one based on the minimum assumptions and the maximum facts available.

The Tennis Scene

Tennis in most countries is based on clubs, although in the UK schools also offer many opportunities to young players and college tennis is particularly strong in the USA.

Clubs

They provide social and competitive play and often cater for other social and sporting activity. Usually coaching is available for adults and juniors and teams play in local leagues. Larger clubs stage major tournaments and representative matches.

All clubs are affiliated to the national governing body, normally via an area (county) association (see Appendix).

Events

Club membership entitles you to enter a nationwide range of open tournaments and age group events

from Under-Eight to Over-Seventy and most areas have Closed Championships for residents.

High Fliers

The prestige events are part of the Grand Prix Circuit and can only be entered by those high on the ATP (Association of Tennis Professionals) and WTA (Women's Tennis Association) computers. Other top players compete in Satellite Tournaments, trying to win enough points to gain Grand Prix entry status. Your county champion would probably have to pre-qualify in order to reach the qualifying rounds of a Satellite event held in your country, so you need to be at least one of the very best juniors in your county to have realistically high ambitions of joining the world elite. However, you may always seek personal excellence.

Coaching and Further Study

Watch top players, probably on TV, particularly noting doubles' movements. See Appendix for advice on further reading and coaching. Realize that deficiencies in your technique reduce your own and widen an opponent's options.

Conclusion

You have opened your eyes to study this book. Open your ears to all the wealth of tennis know-how around you and open your brain to the advice available. Then go on court and open your heart in the way you play your matches.

Appendix

Addresses

The International Tennis Federation
Church Road
Wimbledon
London SW19 5TF
Tel. 01-947 0279

Great Britain

The Lawn Tennis Association (LTA)
Barons Court
London W14 9EG
Tel. 01-385 2366
(Your county association will be affiliated to the LTA. For the address enquire at local library, or recreation department.)

Coaching

The Professional Tennis Coaches' Association (PTCA) will give you details of coaches in your area. The LTA and the PTCA will also give you appropriate details should you wish to train as a coach.
PTCA
21 Glencairn Court
Lansdown Road
Cheltenham
Glos GL50 2NB
Tel. 0242-24701 and 30562

Events and Tournaments

Enquiries to: LTA

Competitors' Nutrition

Write to:
The Sport Nutrition Manager
Wander Ltd
Station Road
King's Langley
Herts WD4 8LJ
Tel. 09277-66122
and request free leaflet, *Nutrition For Games Players.*

Magazines (Great Britain)

Tennis (Monthly)
34 Buckingham Palace Road
London SW1 0RE
Tel. 01-828 4551
Serve and Volley (LTA magazine)

Brief Bibliography

Better Tennis
John Crooke (Kaye & Ward)
For improvement of your stroke technique and all-round game.
The Game of Doubles in Tennis
Bill Talbert and Bruce Old (Gollancz)
For advanced doubles tactics.
Tennis My Way
Martina Navratilova (Penguin)

Index